Jacques Briard

Directeur de recherche au C.

THE MEGALITHS OF BRITTANY

English edition
translated by Juan-Paolo Perre

EDITIONS JEAN-PAUL GISSEROT

Ouessant : Sunrise at the summer solstice. Photo: M. Le Goffic

GLOSSARY

Alignment : A single row or group of rows of menhirs facing the same way often accompanied by other stones arranged in a semi-circle. Also referred to as lines.

Angevin Dolmen : Dolmen typical of the Loire region. Vast in dimension with portico, antechamber and large partitioned chamber.

Angled Dolmen: Dolmen whose entrance corridor comes in at an angle, sometimes at right angles.

Antechamber : Small outer-room leading to the principal chamber of a megalith.

Bronze Age : The period of human culture characterized by the developement of the use of bronze, an alloy of copper and tin, between 2000 and 800 B.C.

Burial Mound : Oblong drystone or earth monument built over graves. May be edged with stones.

Buttressed Gallery grave : Megalith consisting of upright, mutually-supported stone slabs without capstones inclined one against the other to form a chamber.

Cairn : Pile of stones surrounding one or several tombs.

Coffin : Small, megalithic tomb built of stone slabs placed edgewise and covered by flat slabs or buttressed stones.

Cromlech : Circle of monoliths. Use of this term may lead to confusion as it means dolmen in Welsh. See "enclosure".

Dolmen : Term designating various types of megalithic monuments built of stone slabs and thought to be tombs.

Drystone : Building technique characterized by the use of small, flat stones without mortar.

Enclosure : Circular or four-sided area demarcated by menhirs.

Facing : Flagstone or dry-stone construction reinforcing the cairn of a monument.

Gallery grave : A megalithic monument consisting of a large elongated chamber roofed over with flat slabs or lintel stones. It may include partitions, porthole slabs and a small back-room separated from the main chamber by a transversal slab.

Hatchet-Plow : Primitive swing plough using a stone hatchet as ploughshare.

Hemicycle : Semicircle of menhirs.

Megalith : Prehistoric monument made of very large stones.

Megalith with Side Entry : Gallery grave entered through a small passageway perpendicular to the collective, burial chamber.

Menhir : Single upright stone, placed alone or in lines (alignments). May be natural, rough hewn or engraved with symbolic figures.

Neolithic : Of or relating to the latest period of the Stone Age. Prehistoric era, 6000 to 2000 B.C., which saw the developement of farming and the domestication of animals.

Orthostat : Upright stone supporting the flat slabs destined to roof over a monument or circle a mound.

Passage grave : Monument comprising a burial chamber and a lower corridor.

Peristalith: Colonnade of stones surrounding a monument.

Peulvan : Ancient Breton word meaning upright stone. Now replaced by menhir.

Placitre : Area laid out for rituals in front of a megalith.

Portico : Monumental entry of a megalith consisting of a large, horizontal slab supported by two upright stone blocks.

Simple Dolmen : Chamber formed by upright blocks supporting a horizontal stone slab.

Tholos : Dome-shaped burial chamber with small flat stones.

Tombelle : Simple grave marked by a pile of stones.

Transeptal Dolmen : Dolmen with small, lateral rooms on either side of the main chamber.

Tumulus : An artificial hillock or mound built of stones or earth or a combination of the two. May cover tombs or dolmens.

V-shaped Dolmen : Dolmen with a narrow entry widening gradually towards the end of the chamber.

One of the great economic developements of humanity was the acquisition of the techniques of production, domestication of animals and agriculture. This great evolution was called the Neolithic period. Born in the Middle-East, agriculture reached Europe by the Danubian Channel by one side and that of the Mediterranean on the other. Of the danubian elements, recognizable by their pottery were recognizable in Normandy and in the Central West around 5000 B.C. Other fragments decorated by impression or by seashells, typical of the Meditteranean Neolithic period, reached the Atlantic around 5,500 years B.C. at least until the Vendee coast.

Megalithism

Agriculture and cattle-breeding changed the conditions of life. The inhabitants constructed permanent villages, in other words, they "sedentary-ized" themselves. This permitted them to build monuments requiring positioning in the same place for a long period of time as well as elaboration throughout the decades. In addition, the mentality evolved and religion was transformed, oriented especially around the astronomic cults and that of the goddess-mother protector of the dead as well as of the harvests. To give hommage to the new gods, they built large, outdoor temples, whose alignments followed that of the risings and settings of the sun and the moon. For the dead, enormous tombs being constructed of stones: the "megaliths" and "dolmens". They erected, also, stones towards the sky, these were the menhirs that in earlier times were called "peulvans". This happened nearly 5,000 B.C. if one believes in the most modern dating methods of megalithism, like that of radiocarbon dating. During 3,000 years, menhirs and dolmens stood in Brittany as a witness of the religious faith of the populations of farmers who first settled Armorica.

The first dolmens

Tradition has frozen the image of the dolmen as a stone table set upon pillars. In reality, the truth is otherwise. There have been some simple dolmens of this type but at the start of enormous monuments being built. The most attractive examples are the large tumulus with dolmens with antechambers like those of Barnenez, of Guennoc or of Dissignac. In the region of Carnac, some large stretched-out or circular mounds covered some coffins or tombs of rich furniture, these are the tumulus like the Saint-Michel tumulus or the Mane-er-Hroek in Locmariaquer. They erected large menhirs decorated with hatchet-plows in order to then break them and use their pieces to recover the megalithic tombs like the Table of Marchand or the celebrated Gavrinis. These monuments being incessantly modified, enlarged for showing to the world the power of the megalithic tribes.

The recent megaliths

The first dolmens were of a simple design: a corridor lead to a large funeral chamber. Subsequently, around 3,000 B.C., they modified them: the rooms multiplied with the transeptal dolmens or to lateral closets like those of Pornic in the Loire-Atlantique. Some others modified their room by elongating disproportionately. These were the Angevin dolmens or in right angles like the Plates Stones in Locmariaquer.

But also, some other models of tombs developed as a result of the influence of Northern Europe. The gallery graves, like Commana or Tresse, had a new plan with slabs of the same height whereas with the dolmens with antechamber the room was more raised than the entrance corridor. The megaliths with side entries, very close to the gallery graves, had an entry on the side and were surrounded with a large mound like in Saint-Quay-Perros.

On these monuments some representations of goddess-mothers appeared three-dimensionally (pairs of breasts) whereas they were simply engraved on the slabs of the first dolmens. Finally, large monuments with gigantic slabs were built imitating the dolmens of Anjou, like the Roche-aux-Fees in Ille-et-Vilaine. Thus, incessantly, megalithism beared witness to a beautiful vitality throughout its 3,000 years of existence.

Menhirs and alignments

Very early, the principle of the raised stones toward the sky was adopted by the Neolithic people. That was a matter, first of all, of technical exploit because the tallest menhirs could reach 350 tons like in Locmariaquer. Then, one could engrave on the stones religious symbols in use: goddesses, crooks, hatchets or serpents. In addition, they could serve as astronomic landmarks, complicating the system until the realisation of real, outside sanctuaries, these were, first of all, simple lines of menhirs then groups of rows of menhirs, the alignments, finally, of complex constructions where the alignments built-up of circles or enclosures at their end. Carnac is the best example. The profound faith of this population is still present in our day in spite of centuries of destruction and vandelism which has transformed and sometimes destroyed these masterpieces of prehistoric architecture.

Our intention is to mention the most prestigious of these monuments but also to show that which is new of their existence brought to light by modern research. More than a guide, it is intended to act as an incitement to visit the celebrated sites like Carnac, Locmariaquer, but also the multiple joys of megalithism spred throughout L'Argoat to Armor.

Tumiac, butte de Cesar, Morbihan. Photo : J-P Gisserot.

ARZON (peninsula)

The Rhuys peninsula, which closes the southern end of the Golf of Morbihan, has numerous monuments unequally exploited. To the north of Arzon one can cite the Grah Niol dolmen which, under its present undergrowth, is hidden some interesting, engraved slabs. Some lowered mounds like the one of Bilgroix were those neolithic tombs without rooms. But two monuments are particularly celebrated, Tumiac and le Petit-Mont.

TUMIAC BUTTE DE CESAR

District of Arzon, Morbihan

On arriving near Arzon, one can not help but notice this impressive mound of 50 meters in diameter and 15 meters high. It is said that Ceasar observed from here the naval battle which saw the Romans as the conquerers of the Venetes as a result of the lull in the winds. The monument was searched "in crater" by the pioneers of the last century (1853) who threw out their earth to the sides. They found in the depths, a small, megalithic room with engraved walls and rich furnishings of smooth axing and pendants made of precious rocks. One goes down to the room by a stairway which was recently closed for danger of collapsing. Its difficult restoration must wait. Tumiac belonged to the great tumulus "carnaceens", sepulchers of the elite neolithic people around 4,000 B.C., like those of Saint-Michel to Carnac and of Mane-er-Hroek to Locmariaquer.

LE PETIT MONT

District of Arzon, Morbihan

To the south of Arzon, after the port of Crouesty on the granite cliff, the Petit-Mont doninates the sea. This monument, disturbed by the roman occupation, excavated from 1864 and restored in 1906, had trials and tribulations when in 1943 the Germans destroyed a room in order to install a blockhouse in it's place. Its patient restoration by J. Lecornec from 1979 to 1988 allowed it to be given an image conforming more to its original architecture and to be an interesting monument to visit to this day. This enormous cairn of 60 meters in length, 46 meters in width and 6 to 7 meters in height is comprised of several dolmens with antechambers which one in the South-West shows remarkable engravings: axings in circles or "sun", undulating signs, fitted axings, etc. It displays an entrance portico. Its furnishings, unfortunately dispersed, comprise some axes and some neolithic ceramics but also statuettes of Venus from the times when the Romans had transformed the dolmen en "fanum" or sanctuary. On the outside, the facings and foothills in drystone spread out by place on eight levels. This large, complex megalith was built progressively on two cairns successively making at least three dolmens. In the center there exists a german bunker converted to the most pacific role of documentary center !

MENHIR DE KERMAILLARD

District of Sarzeau

Several menhirs are known on the peninsula (Grah Niol) but the one of Kermaillard-Le Net, between Arzon et Sarzeau, merits a visit. Known under the name of Scalehir or "The Lump of Butter" it was a block laying on it's side of 5 meters long representing a game of cupules (small, round holes). Raised in 1985, it revealed a worked surface of remarkable simplicity with two beautiful engravings:a squared, stylized representation of the "goddess-mother" and a quarter-moon, bringing to mind neolithic, religious symbols of great value.

Menhir of Kermaillard. Photo F. de Lesdain.

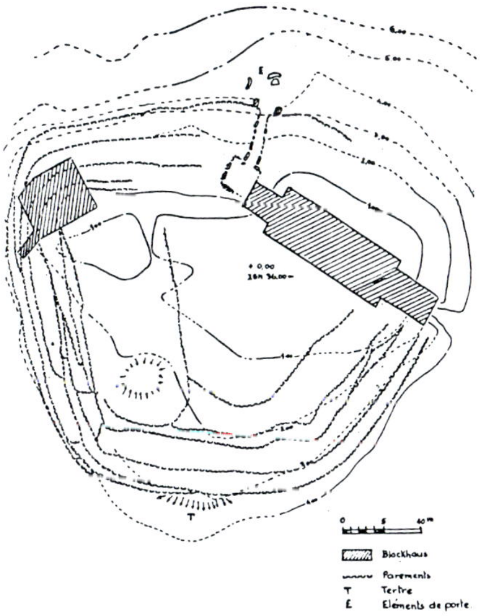

The Petit-Mont in Arzon. Photos J. Lecornec, P. Avré.

General view of Barnenez . Photo J.-P. Gisserot

BARNENEZ-CARN GUENNOC

Whereas one believed to know everything about Brittany's dolmens, the great salvaging excavations conducted on 3 coastal sites: Finistère, Barnenez, Carn and Guennoc, have upset the knowledge of megalithism in Amorica if not world-wide. Thus, new structures, tholos and exterior facings have been discovered. Interesting furnishings associated with some engravings, showed an original aspect especially with regards to the radiocarbon dates obtained proving that these monuments could have been erected around 4,000 or 5,000 B.C., some 2,000 years before the Pyramids. Finally, a restoration specimen copy brought on by the excavation allows visitors a glimpse of these prehistoric treasures of the archeological inheritance of Finistère.

BARNENEZ

District of Plouézoch, Finistère

The tumulus is found at the top of the peninsula of Kernélehen, on the right bank of the estuary of the Morlaix river. The monument is protected by a wire fencing (guided visitation).

This giant megalith is a restoration. In the begining it was, as a result of falling rocks, a shapeless mass of 90 meters long, 40

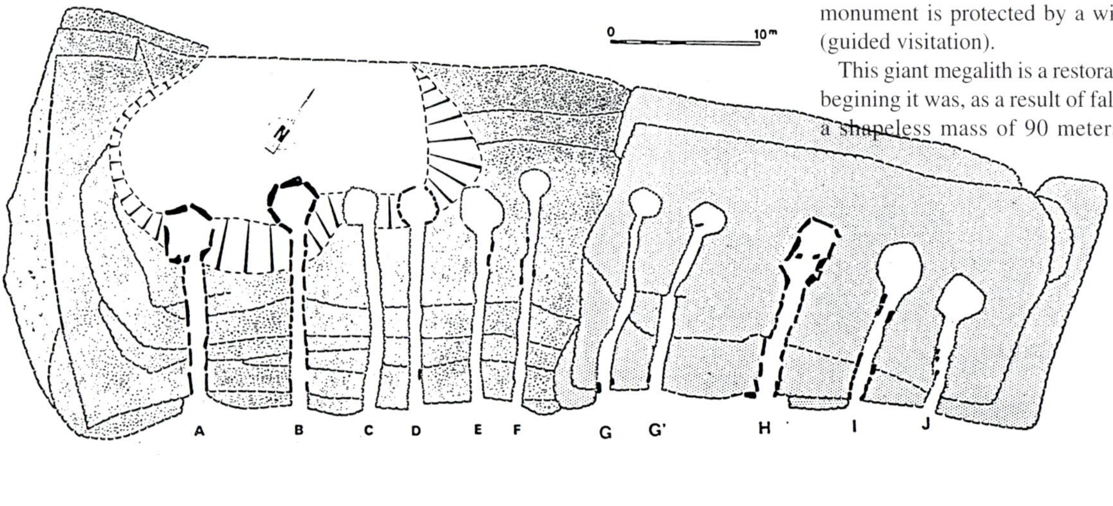

meters wide and 6 to 7 meters high. It had been slightly forgotten by the archeologists who vaguely labeled it as an entrenchment. It was not the only tumulus of it's kind as another tumulus more to the North, was also an imposing mass of granite blocks and rocks of the area, the dolorite. What a godsend for a builder of local, touristic routes! For this reason, around 1950, the tumulus became quarries of sorts. The northern tumulus was largely ripped open and its large, central dolmen destroyed. The central dolmen, the one one sees today, was struck upon by an opencast quarry bringing up to date five dolmenic chambers which subsequently were left open (as a sort of "cut-away drawing") after strengthening finally to better allow comprehension of their internal architecture.

The salvaging excavation and the restoration of Barnenez lasted some dozen years. The dolmens were extricated from the west to the east and designated by letters alphabetically from A to J. A "forgotten one" discovered afterwards was therefore christened "G1" In fact, the Barnenez tumulus is made up of two cairns (stone structures), one boxed-in by the other. The first one contains dolmens J, I, H, G1 and G. It is colored slightly darker, composed essentially of green dolerite from the local subsoil. The second cairn is of a lighter color because in order to construct it, granite from the small island of Sterec, situated more to the north, was mined and transported 1 to 2 km. Tightly joined together to the first one, it is made up of dolmens F, E, D, C, B and A. In fact, the order of discovery by the archeologist was opposite to the order of their construction. Those here are the dolmens with antechambers built on drystone walls, with sometimes pillars supporting them and covered with granite slabs.

The chambers are, for the most part, in tholos, namely, in the form of an oven or pointed hive with parts made up of slabs of shale or in tablets of granite. However, tombs B and H consist of chambers made of flat, granite slabs. The chambers in tholos: A and D, incorporate, against the base of the tholos, large slabs erected on foothills.

The group, therefore, is made up of 11 dolmens (five for cairn 1 and six for cairn 2) It appears organized around dolmen H, by double chamber, ornamented with engravings: arches, axings, undulating signs (the sea?) which could have played the role of central temple in the middle of the funeral group. Other dolmens also have engravings : U-shaped signs (undoubtably of cattle) at the entrance of dolmen A, and a beautiful figure of the "goddess-mother ", a rectangular badge with "hair" under a slab at the entrance of the chamber of dolmen J.

The datings of Barnenez suggest that it was constructed some 6,700 years ago for the former part and 6,400 years before this moment now for the more recent, western part. The increase of the population necessitated, undoubtably, this enlargement. The collected pottery shows that it was in usage for several millennium, until the dawn of the Bronze Age around 2,000 B.C.

It's enormous mass (55 115 imperial tons of stones) is organized from the exterior. It

The face-side of Barnenez. Photo J-P Gisserot

Dolmen in tholos of Barnenez. Photo J. Briard

Barnenez, goddess of dolmen J . Photo J. Briard

Barnenez, dolmen B . Photo J. Briard

is an immense funeral vessel with it's bow prepared with slabs and a structure in successive tiers which comparisons were sometimes made, improperly, to the Pyramids of Egypt or the Ziggourats of Mesapotamia. But, of course, leave it to the first neolithic farmers to be the first to sow the first wheat fields in Brittany.

Barnenez witnesses, with eloquence,the faith which drove the country population but the monuments were also the symbolic witness of the power and the population's grasp on the territory which they controlled.

CARN

District of Ploudalmézeau, Finistère

This little island is accessible only at low tide today. It is comprised of a beautiful group of three dolmens with antechambers relatively well-conserved in spite of the establishing of german blockhouses at the time of the second war. Legend had it that

Tumulus of Carn Island. Photo J. Briard

this may have been the palace of the king of Carn from the ears of donkeys...In 1954, a first dolmen with antechambers in tholos was discovered there intact, then some subsequent countyside permitted them to add a second dolmen with antechamber and a third, curiously with double chambers. All of it was restored.

The current monument shows the same system of outside facings as in Barnenez. It gave way to beautiful, round-bottomed pottery, silex blades, and charcoal confirming the former dating of these monuments near 4 to 5,000 B.C. But the monument was still used around 2,500 B.C. and as proof, a curious "collerette bottle" of a type found in Northern Europe. Then, it seems to have been filled-in at the front by an enormous blockade, more than a meter high, which protected the sepulchers until the 20th century.

GUENNOC

Guennoc Island (or Gaignoc)
District of Landéda, Finistère

This site is the most difficultly accessible to the localities of reefs of L'Aber Vracht. But the visit, by embarking by small boat starting from the bay of Prat-ar-Coum, famed for it's oysters, allows the discovery of an archeological group comprising a series of neolithic tumulus and a medival hermitage. It is an exceptional site inhabited today, solely by a population of seagulls defending fiercely their territory in the company of small rabits feeding on seaweed.

The island was known for its dolmens and its prehistoric discoveries where a deposit of bronze objects showing that around 800 B.C. it could have been a counter for the trade of Amorican tin/pewter.

The Guennoc dolmens are regrouped in numbers from 3 to 6 on four cairns distributed on the backbone of the island. These are the dolmens with antechambers, in tholos, more rarely in slabs, which have lost their cover. For this reason, one can observe most often their circular chamber cut at mid-height. At the entrance of several chambers a small slab of slate constructed and sized schematically in human silhouette. It is the goddess of the dead and of the harvest who keep a watchful eye on their sepulchers. The dolmens of Guennoc have delivered an abundance of neolithic furnishings, pottery and silex. Some slabs show engravings very much eroded (U-shaped signs). Certain dolmens have been destroyed at the time of the Gauls (a number of pottery) in order to be transformed into residences. Subsequently, the island was a hermitage, a sheep farm and during the war of 1939-1945, a base of repatriation for English pilots.

Dolmen of Guernnoc. Photo J. Briard

Barnenez, Carn, Guennoc (the B.C.G. of P.-R. Giot) show all the richness of North Finistère's megalithism and the abundance of the monuments established on the coasts for economic reasons (fishing, silex, diverse stones, outside communications), Nevertheless, some Neolithic people ventured towards the interior during this time as is shown by the tumulus of Ty Floch in Saint-Thois with chambers in tholos containing "bone packets" a little like the Middle Age ossuaries. This precious eyewitness shows well the role in the funerals that these monuments played built from 5,000 B.C. and used for 3 millennium.

BROCELIANDE (forest of)

The Brocéliande forest is one of the highest places in American legend. Located there is the Secret Bridge where the fairy Viviane vowed her love to Merlin before being sealed up in an invisible cloud, the Valley of No Return where Morgan imprisonned his unfaithful lovers or even the Comper Pond where Viviane raised Lancelot of the Lake on a place constructed before his eyes. Hence, a number of megalithic monuments of the forest were attributed to the Arthurian heros and are still, to our day, the "receptacle of souls". The Tomb of Merlin is the last relic of a gallery grave situated near the Marelles pond to the east of the forest, the symbolic place where those fans of the heros of the Round Table, meet each year. Viviane's Hotié is a megalithic coffin considered by legend to be the residences of the fairy Viviane. The Brocéliande monuments, reported primarily in the 19th century, have been rediscovered recently thanks to the impassione members of the Moulin Association of Châtenay and also following fires which periodically devestated the forest. A series of searches led from 1982 to 1985 permitted the recognition therein of the most characteristic monuments.

THE HOTIE OF VIVIANE

District of Paimpont, île-et-Vilaine

One must, in order to find this House of Viviane (in earlier times called the Tomb of the Druids) go back up into the deep forest by the village of Beauvais, towards the moor of Ranco. After having left the last houses of the Guette and the last culivated farms one crosses the crest of red shale, perfumed by the asphodel in the Spring, to come upon a small clearing where up shoots the megalithic coffin of the Hotie of Viviane, above the smaller legendary valley in the Valley of No Return.

The Hotie of Viviane
Photo : J. Briard

The Hotie of Viviane. Photo : J. Briard

The Hotié of Viviane is a megalithic tomb constructed with large slabs of red slate from the area numbering twelve. The covering destroyed by the treasure hunters in earlier times, has disappeared. The tomb measures on the inside 2.90 meters in length for a maximum of 1.60 meters in width. A slab slightly lower, on the southern side, allowed entrance in order to deposit the dead. The excavation permitted aquaintance, around the coffin, with a tumulus matching up with small slabs of shale. This too fragile structure had to be filled in after the excavation but one can notice the largest stones of the entourage. The Hotié of Viviane has brought forth some nice axings cut into the dolerite of Plussulien, Côtes d'Armor, some millstones, strikers, some Silex and pieces of pottery of the final Neolithic, agreeing with the radiocarbon dating obtained (3,355 to 2,890 B.C.)

It is a somewhat exceptional example of contemporary megalithic coffins with gallery graves more numerous in this era, particularly along the Paimpont forest. A monument of the same type is known in Grand-Champ, Morbihan, but is unfortunately destroyed.

THE GARDEN OF THE MONKS - LE JARDIN AUX MOINES

District of Néant-sur-Yvel, Morbihan

At the crossing of the route, leading from Tréhorenteuc to Mauron and the one going from Paimpont to Néant-sur-Yvel, is found a series of long tumulus among them the "Mound of the Tombs" in going to Mauron and the large round mound called "The Round Mound" in the woods going towards Tréhorenteuc. The Garden of the Monks was decreed in the last century as a "round bordered with menhirs". Legend interprets it as the petrification of a cursed shrine leading to Toussaint by the terrible Lord Gastern de Tréhorenteuc. Lords and bad monks were transformed into white stones at the place of their sins. The Garden of the Monks is in reality a neolithic mound lined with white pudding-stone blocks on the northern part, blocks springing from at least 3 km, and some slabs of red shale from the local subsoil, alternating with blocks of quartz on it's southern part. The group measures 25 meters in length with 6 meters in width. The monument contains two internal, transversal separations localized in it's northern part and which can show successive enlargements.

The collected furnishings are composed of ceramics of the final Neolithic, around 3,000-2,500 B.C. It was subsequently reused as a grave or sanctuary. A small foyer, dated 2,000 B.C. has given us silex arrowheads corresponding to this dating perhaps being the beginning of the Bronze Age.

The Garden of the Monks is not unique in Brittany, of such monuments, probably graves of a non-megalithic structure, are known as well in the Loire-Atlantique (Le Brétineau in Guérande) as in the Morbihan

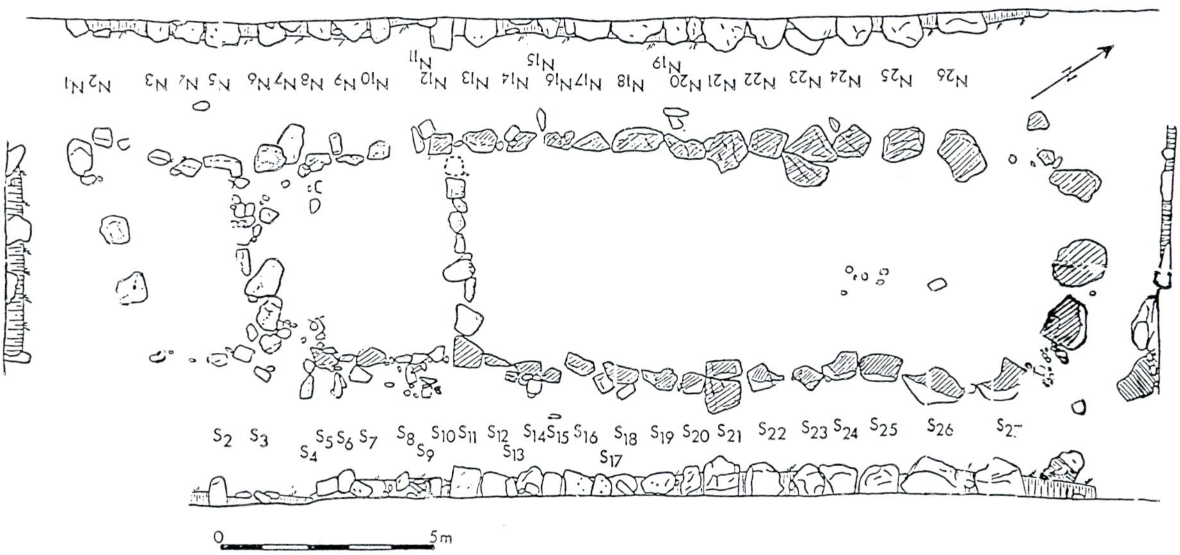

(Le Manio in Carnac) or the Côtes d'Armor (Notre-Dame-de-Lorette au Quillio). They show of the extreme diversification of Amorican megalithism. Here, the graves were of simple heaps of stones in the interior of the monument.

The Garden of the Monks . Photo J. Briard

Page at left : The Grave of the Giants.
Photo J. Briard

THE GRAVE OF THE GIANTS
LE TOMBEAU DES GÉANTS

District of Campénéac, Morbihan

The Grave of the Giants, in former times called "the Rock of the Old Dame" (the Witch), is found to the west of the Lucas Cross, above the village of Beauvais, in the morbihanese territory of the Brocéliande forest. It is a large, megalithic, closed vault where the longitudinal walls are formed of two fat blocks of red shale of the area of 4.5 meters in length and 1 meter in height. The transversal walls are of smaller walls of drystone. At the end, the vault measures 3 meters in length and 1.30 meters in width. The covering slab, displaced to the side by treasure hunters a century ago is of shale. 8 meters to the north of the monument is found a reclining menhir of 4 meters in length.

This grave belongs to a series of sepulchers of the former Bronze, around 1,500 B.C. It was probably constructed by using the stones of a neolithic alignment, first constructed on the same spot. Furthermore, such alignments, oriented north-south, are known in the Paimpont forest like the Drette Stone 2km east of the Chateau of Comper.

The circumference of the Brocéliande Forest is completely made up of a series of gallery graves. One can cite the one, ruined, of the Rocher in Concoret, the one in Brousses Noires near the Grave of Merlin in Paimpont or still, a little further away, the gallery graves of Hino or of the Ville Bouquet in Ploërmel. This last one was made the object of an excavation campaign in 1985. Pollen analysis has revealed traces of farming (grain) whereas in the Brocéliande Forest only the deforestation, perhaps for cattle-breeding and housing, were discovered.

La Ville Bouquet. Photo J. Briard

CARNAC-ERDEVEN
Morbihan

The alignments

The alignments of Carnac are among the sacred giants of American cultural tourism along the same stature as the Mont-Saint-Michel. This is not without it's problems. The stampede of an immense cohort of visitors has eroded the floors and worked loose the menhirs dangerously. Moreover, quite often the touristic cars halt only at the principal groups at Carnac, permitting the time only for the new-comers to take a picture of little Johnny or Suzie at the foot or sommet of one of these prestigious stones. And they go away again ignoring that therein lies a complex grouping of monuments which start not at Carnac but more to the west at Erdeven to form a gigantic cultural grouping on more than 5 km. In addition, if the lines of menhirs are visited, often one ignores the megalithic enclosures or "cromlechs" which complete each group of alignments at their end. It is true that these enclosures of menhirs were often destroyed or are hidden in our day by modern constructions. Much ink has been split over the alignments for two centuries. The first ones revealed like those of La Sauvagère in 1755 showed their prefered orientation bound to the rising of the sun and one sees there very early on an astronomic cult in formation. The risings pointed out by A. Thom permitted the retracing of the typical layout of an alignment making up some dozen lines of menhirs with, at each end, an enclosure often elliptical, the "megalithic egg". Series of perpendicular lines to the main alignments completed the organization of these monuments which were without a doubt built in the Middle Neolithic Age, around 4,000 to 3,000 B.C.

KERZERHO
District of Erdeven, Morbihan

These alignments were truncated by the establishment of the road leading from Erdeven to Quiberon. The form a group of more than 2km including several thousand stones on 65 meters in width. Today, one can see that which remains there 1km to the south of Erdeven; to the right of the road some large menhirs of which one ornamented with cupules are probably the remains of one of the enclosures. To the left of the road exists ten or so lines of menhirs oriented east-west. But the most interesting of the Kerzerho group is complementing line which is directed towards the North and makes up some very handsome elements of which one of water, on it's side, was most certainly baptised the "Table of Sacrifice". The influence of Romanticism is still alive!

Further south of Erdeven one must notice a small grouping of alignments: the 6 menhirs of the Vieux Moulin to the east of the road and the menhirs of Sainte-Barbe, relics of a group more important in earlier times.

Three views of the alignments of Kerzerho. Photo J-P Gisserot

Menec Alignment . Photo: J. Briard

THE MENEC

District of Carnac, Morbihan

This is the most beautiful group of alignments. The main part of its western megalithic enclosure is conserved making it necessary to go into the village. The enclosure of 90 meters by 70 meters counts yet a series of 70 joined menhirs in particular to the North-West. One sees the difference between the menhirs with enclosures joined one to the another and those of the main alignment isolated one from another. The alignments make up 12 lines of menhirs on a length which varies from 116 meters to the west to 63 meters to the east. The menhirs are arranged by decreasing size starting from the west. They are numbered from 1,099 to 1,165 meters. The eastern megalithic enclosure, more dismantled, is lost in the moor but is still obvious. A small complementary line of menhirs runs from the alignment towards the North.

The alignments show a light inflection at mid-length, there where passes at the moment a road, which shifts the orientation of the megalithic enclosures. For A. Thom and A. Burl that permitted them to be orientated following the rising and setting of the sun in the summer and winter solstices. A true openair calender.

Page to right:
Kermario alignment. Photo J-P Gisserot

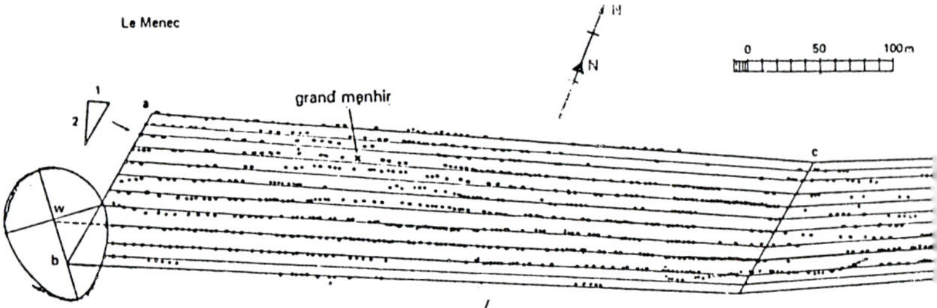

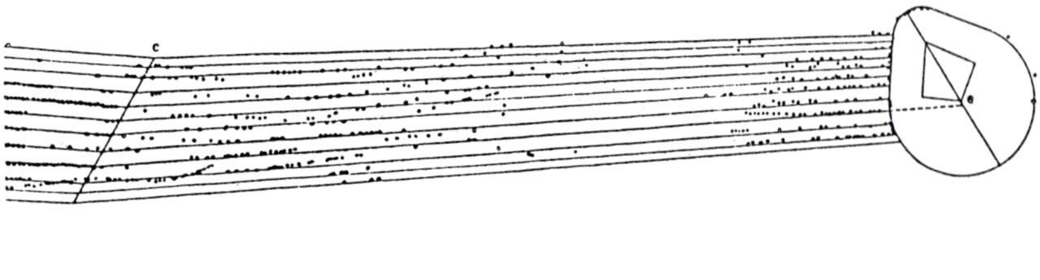

At left : *two views of Kermario.*
Photos : J-P Gisserot

KERMARIO

District of Carnac, Morbihan

If you park your car in the Kermario parking lot, know that you are at the site of the missing, western, megalithic enclosure! For this reason, the alignment abruptly starts its 10 to 12 lines of 982 menhirs spread-out over 1.2 km in length. It should be said that, as with the other alignments, many of the menhirs had fallen. Zacharie Le Rouzic revealed them by marking on them a small pellet of red cement at their base. If you look for it you can note the sizeable number of stones reset up! The menhirs of Kermario went up hill and down dale, crossing a river, unfortunately the ones that "bathed themselves" there have been pulled-up from the reserve of modern water. To the east, some alignments exist as the remains of a megalithic enclosure. The alignment is bordered by an attractive dolmen with antechamber, without a doubt, older.

KERLESCAN

District of Carnac, Morbihan

This megalithic group reveals a very beautiful western enclosure of a quadrangular form of 78 m by 74 m. The eastern side contains 18 joined stones parting from the main alignment where the 13 lines spread out in a fan shape over 355 m, uniting more than sixty stones. To the north of the alignment is found an attractive menhir which displays a long funeral mound constructed at its feet. 1 km to the west of the Kerlescan enclosure is situated the "Manio Quadrilateral" with another large menhir, but this monument has been very restored in modern times.

To right : *Menhir of Kerlescan.*
Photo : J-P Gisserot

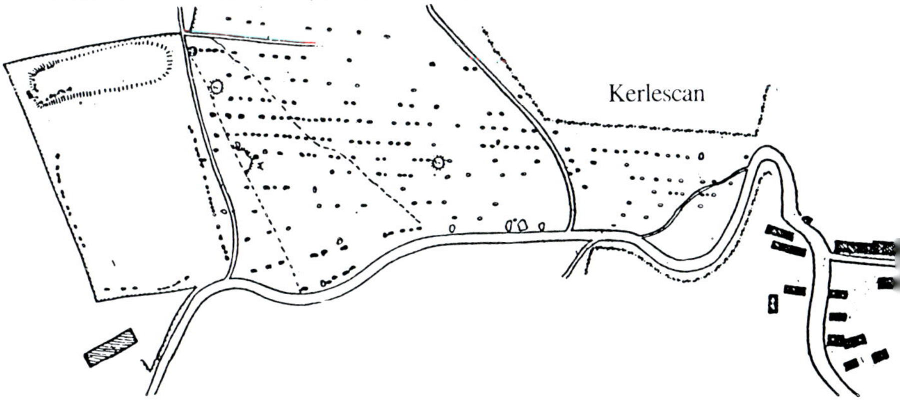

THE SMALL MENEC

Disrtict of Carnac, Morbihan

This one is often a "forgotten one" of the road of megaliths which stretch the Menec, Kermario and Kerlescan. In fact, in order to reach it one must not go towards Locmariaquer after the alignments of Kerlescan but go up again towards the north and at 200m go in again to the woods to the right. The place is besides somewhat swampy. The Small Menec is somewhat original with 8 lines of menhirs arranged fan-shaped in length and hold hundreds of stones. Earlier, they were more than 250 but in the middle of the last century the administration, not very sensitive to their "barbaric" charm, exploited them in order to build the Lighthouse of Belle-Ile!The fan-shaped arrangement is here without a doubt connected to a will to diversify the astronomic designs. It is a witness still to the variety of megalithic constructions. Besides, it is not possible that Kerlescan and the Small Menec primitively took part of the same group. The construction of villages and the road had separated them from modern times.

CARNAC-ERDEVEN
Dolmens

The extraordinary concentration of dolmens in the region of Carnac witness well that there was an exceptional center of megalithism there. One can only mention here, of course, a few of these monuments showing their variety, the large, giant mounds known as carnacéens up to the dolmens with lateral closets in passing by the classic dolmens with antechambers. In addition, the Carnac Museum, renovated in a modern fashion, would be for every visitor an excellent point of departure.

The Saint-Michel Tumulus . Photo J-P. Gisserot

TUMULUS SAINT-MICHEL
District of Carnac, Morbihan

This giant of 125m in length, 50m in width and 10m in height is the most imposing of the mounds known as carnacéens. In 1862, the prefect of Morbihan, intriqued, enlisted R. Galles to excavate there. After having pierced a bed of stones, the archeologist discovered a mass of strengthened vases then a dolmen, a sort of internal crypt, where therein was found very beautiful axings in jadeite and in fibrolite, some pearls of callaïs and some silex tools. In 1900, Zacharie Le Rouzic, who dedicated his life to the salvage of the Carnac monuments, explored the Saint-Michel tumulus by a wooded gallery leading from the east. He discovered, thus, a second dolmen and a series of some fifteen small irregular coffins containing axings, neolithic pottery and silex blades. Today, one can visit the monument by the reinforced excavation galleries but one must not forget that these are artificial entrances. The monument had therefore a central chamber and a series of coffins covered by the enormous mass of the mound. Only the dolmen situated to the east could be eventually reused. Some radiocarbon datings suggest that the monument could have been used from 6,000 to 3,000 B.C. These enormous sepulchers could have been reserved for the leading aristocracy. In Carnac, the Moustoir tumulus, length of 90m by 40m in width, belongs to the same series.

TUMULUS OF KERCADO
District of Carnac, Morbihan

This handsome dolmen with antechamber below tumulus is found on private grounds, to the south of the Kermario alignments, but are easily visited by ringing a bell at the entrance of the chateau. It has as its particularity being surrounded by a circle of menhirs. It contains some beautiful slabs engraved including a cuting in a badge shape, probably a stylization of the goddess-mother.

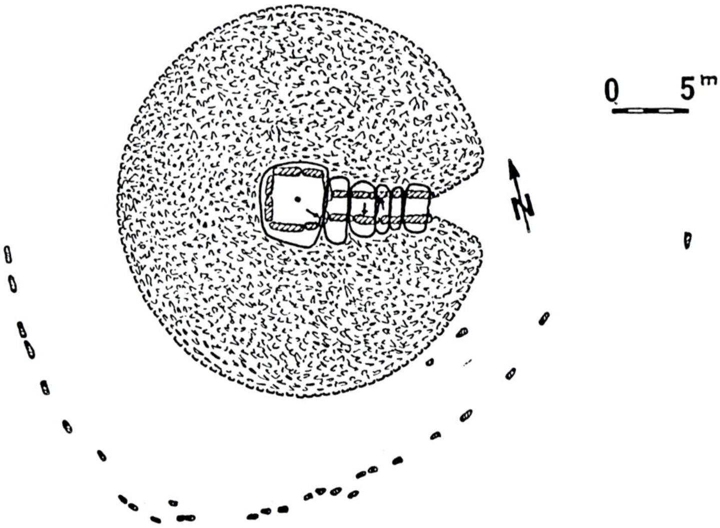

DOLMEN OF KERMARIO

District of Carnac, Morbihan

At the southern border of the start of the Kermarian alignments is found a dolmen with antechamber still quite imposing but stripped of its mound. It is probably anterior to the alignments. Pearls of amber have been collected there. Numerous other groups of dolmens with antechambers are known in Carnac like the group of three dolmens of Mané Kerioned, curiously arranged in a U-shape, the central element being perpendicular to the two others.

Two views of the Kermario dolmen. Photo : J.-P. Gisserot

At left : two views of the Rondossec dolmens. Photo J-P Gisserot

DOLMENS OF RONDOS SEC

District of Plouharnel, Morbihan

Situated just at the north entrance of Plouharnel, this large circular cairn was explored beginning in 1849 by the Society for the exploration of gold of the dolmens! Collected there are two necklaces of gold formed with straps of a portuguese type dating 2,000 B.C. The southern dolmen is a small monument cornered between the facings of the cairn and the central dolmen with a large chamber in the form of a bottle, with a shrunken entrance. The northern dolmen is a rectangular chamber with a small lateral closet put against its southern side. Its corridor is very long (11m). The major part of the covering slabs remain having sometimes rectangular notches due to the attempts of the cutting-up of the quarry workers! The State's purchase of the monument saved it from destruction. Aside from the golden necklaces buried late the monument has brought forth classic neolithic furnishings, vases, nice axings and silex.

DOLMEN OF CRUCUNO

District of Plouharnel, Morbihan

The village of Crucuno is located midway, 1km to the east, of the Erdeven-Plouharnel route. It possesses a dolmen stripped of its mound and lacking its entrance corridor. And yet, what remains is one of the most spectacular ones with its enormous covering slabs. Within the village it served as a barn, of refuge to a simple spirit and its current environment often has room for improvement with its coverings in fibrocement or a variety of rubbish. A former description by W. Lukis in 1864 indicates that the monument possessed a long corridor which he gave a total length of 27m.

To the east of the dolmen, in the middle of the fields, stands the "Crucuno quadrilateral" made up of 22 menhirs. At the moment, the rectangle is perfectly oriented to the points of the compass but it should be said that a modern restoration is perhaps at the origin of this too-precise orientation.

The Crucuno dolmen. Photo J.P.Gisserot

Two views of the Mané Groh dolmen. Photo J-P Gisserot

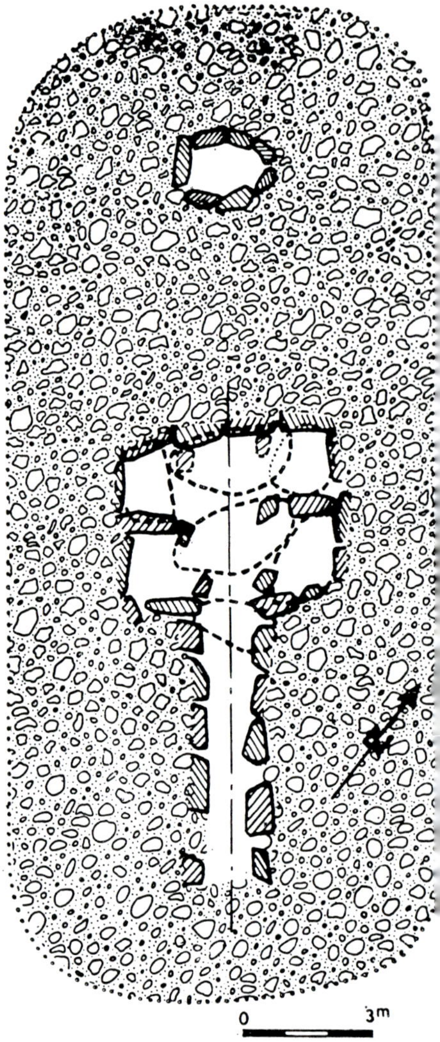

The Mané-Groh Dolmen; general plan by Z. Le Rouzic and J. L'Helgouach.

DOLMEN OF MANE GROH

District of Erdeven, Morbihan

After passing the village of Crucuno one reaches a small wooded area in 1km. At left is found a mound with a handsome dolmen who's long corridor of 6m leads to a funeral space divided into 4 cells arranged symmetrically 2 by 2 around its central corridor. The entrance is the south-east. The covering is very incomplete. The excavation by Z. LeRouzic in 1920 showed that it had a small coffin in the western part of the mound, behind the dolmen. Another monument of the same type is found in Erdeven at the Mané-Bras.

These monuments date to the recent Neolithic, they were used until about 2,000 B.C. (bell-shaped pottery). they are somewhat rare in Brittany although one might associate them with the sepulchers with compartmental chambers of Southern Finistère (the Forest-Fouesnant).

COLPO-LANVAUX MOORS

The granite of the Lanvaux moors was used by the builders of megaliths to lift menhirs, dolmens and gallery graves. These monuments are often difficult to reach in the middle of the moor. Nevertheless, one can visit there several of them like the menhirs of Moustoir-Ac with the giant one of

Tumulus of Larcuste. Photo : Jacques Briard

6.50 m in height carring figurations of hooks and crescents or even the beautiful megalithic grouping of Larcuste.

DOLMENS OF LARCUSTE

District of Colpo, Morbihan

At some twenty kilometers north of Vannes,the village of Larcuste, to the west of the Locminé road, is dominated by a small hill on which is found two handsome cairns restored around 1972 by J. Lecornec and J. L'Helgouach. The monuments are protected by a fencing, which it is necessary to walk around, and appears in a distance, as a result of badly-maintained vegetation, like that of a large brushwood in the middle of cultivated fields.

The northern tumulus, Colpo I, has two dolmens with antechambers with a cairn with facings. A dolmen possesses a large covering slab, the other must have been a tholos, collapsed nowadays.

The southern tumulus, Colpo II, has six little chambers distributed on either side of the central corridor, 9.70 m in length. This dolmen with transeptal structure had been dated by radiocarbon testing at 4,400 B.C. for its former phase. And the numerous pottery, of which bowls with hollow feet have been collected in Colpo, certain ones in the graves and others in offerance in front of the monument. This grouping shows that megalithism reached inside Brittany episodical ly during the oldest periods of its development.

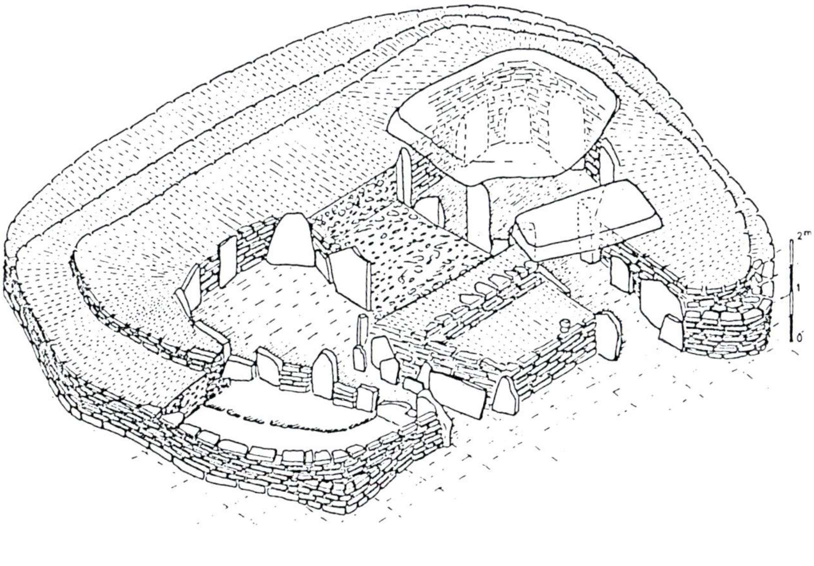

CROZON (peninsula)

The megaliths have been very irregularly conserved according to the regions. Sometimes, the destruction is multiplied from the last century. The peninsula of Crozon, one of the furthest points going towards the sea, was one of the privileged places where prehistoric men had multiplied there astronomic temples. They are well-known from the ancient descriptions given by authors such as the Chevalier de Fréminville or Bachelot de la Pylaie who have given some good sketches of these groupings which were still impressive around 1830. In 1910, the commander A. Devoir, who assigned himself to their salvage, could only pick out but some few relics much diminished by the actions of the quarrymen.

THE ALIGNMENTS OF LAGATJAR

District of Camaret, Finistère

The three lines of menhirs of this alignment have been restored in 1928 with a tad too much rigidity in its uprightness. One can count a hundred or so stones. The longest of the alignments, composed of 42 stones, is oriented at 30°. It its north-east end begins a series of 13 blocks of white quartz and to the south-west the third line aligns 17 large menhirs. This group shows that large alignments analogous to those of Carnac have existed on the peninsula of Crozon. The former descriptions of the monuments of Leuré and of Landouadec, to the north of Crozon, gathered more than 300 menhirs. One can count there at least a few unmatched elements. The ancient engravings represented some groups of completed alignments of circles of stones notably in Landouadec.Another interesting site is Lostmach point, barred and butressed entranchment with a double ditch protecting it towards the continent. Also there are some erected stones which are the relics of an astronomical megalithic ensemble. To the contrary, the system of rectangular enclosures of Ty-ar-Churé near Morgat is probably a protection of a residence of the Bronze Age analogous to those of England.

The alignments of Lagatjar

DOLMEN OF ROSTUDEL

District of Crozon-Morgat, Finistère

Numerous small simple dolmens have existed on the peninsula of Crozon and on its neighboring territory in the districts of Argol, Saint-Nic or still on the sacred hill of Menez-Hom. 5 km south of Morgat, near the hamlet of Keravel, the Rostudel dolmen is still impressive with its large covering slab perched on three pillars. It is, again, a monument having lost its tumulus and its eventual entranceway, but it is a witness to the presence of complementary funeral buildings of the alignments. It well seems that this type of simple dolmen had been nevertheless quite frequent in the region.

Dolmen of Rostudel
Photo : J.P. Gisserot.

DISSIGNAC KERBOURG PORNIC

A number of megaliths are found in the Loire-Atlantique, forming original groups like the ones among the transeptal dolmens with lateral closets. They are abundant in the Pornic region. To the north of the Loire la Brière shows also a great variety of megaliths. Certain ones, buried in the peat-bog, are interesting examples of the variation of the water level like the Pierre-Blanche in Trignac, the Hélé in Donges or the Roche aux Moines hidden amongst the reeds of the Clos d'Orange in Saint-Lyphard. Relics of neolithic habitations have been found on the "islands" like the Butte aux Pierres. Around la Brière some large megalithic monuments attest to the importance and to the spirtuality of the neolithic population.

DOLMEN DE KERBOURG

District of Saint-Lyphard, Loire-Atlantique

It is at 6 km the the north-east of Guérande that sign "druidic stones" signals the beautiful dolmen of Kerbourg, length of 8 m. The slabs of its corridor raise progressively to the circular chamber of 3 m in diameter covered by an enormous table of granite. It is the type of example of a classic dolmen stripped of it's tumulus which had primatively covered it. A variety of pottery have been collected there including the "bell-shaped" vases which show that it was still in usage around 2,000 B.C.

Near to this monument another dolmen disrupted by treasure hunters is nothing more than a "cup of little stones". The group of megaliths is completed by a handsome white menhir in quartz which rises 500 m to the south of the Kerbourg dolmen.

TUMULUS OF DISSIGNAC

District of Saint-Nazaire, Loire-Atlantique

This attractive tumulus, situated 5 km to the west of Saint-Nazaire, covers two dolmens each one equipped with a corridor of 11 m in length leading to a central chamber. The smallest is covered with a granite slab bearing engravings of hooks and hatchet-plows recalling the figuration on the dolmens of Morbihan. The Dissignac tumulus was excavated and restored recently by J. L'Helgouach who enlightened us to several stages of construction: around 4,500 B.C. two dolmens were constructed side by side. Their orientation was calculated in order to observe the rising of the sun at the winter solstice following the axis of the corridors. During a second phase, the monument was enlarged by ellongating its corridors. The primitive facade, composed of slabs, was

Dolmen of Kerbourg. Photo : J.P. Gisserot

The tumulus of Dissignac

reinforced by small walls of drystone giving the structure in tiers such that it is reconstituted today. An abundance of pottery collected in the interior shows a long use of the monument from the ancient Neolithic period around 4,500 to the final Neolithic period near 2,500 B.C.

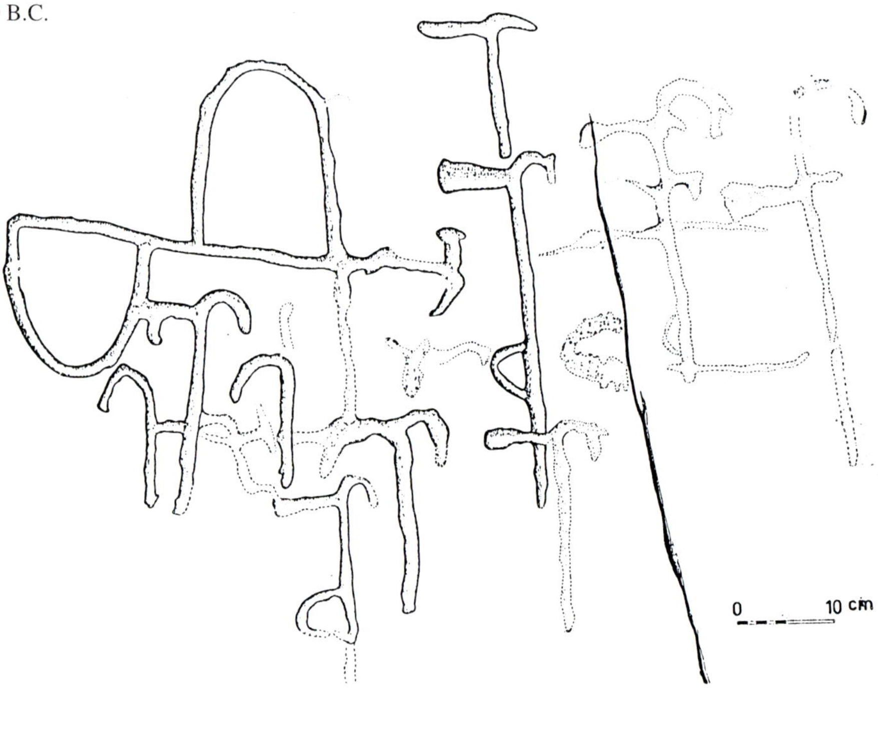

Tumulus of the Mousseaux. Photo P. Réveleau)

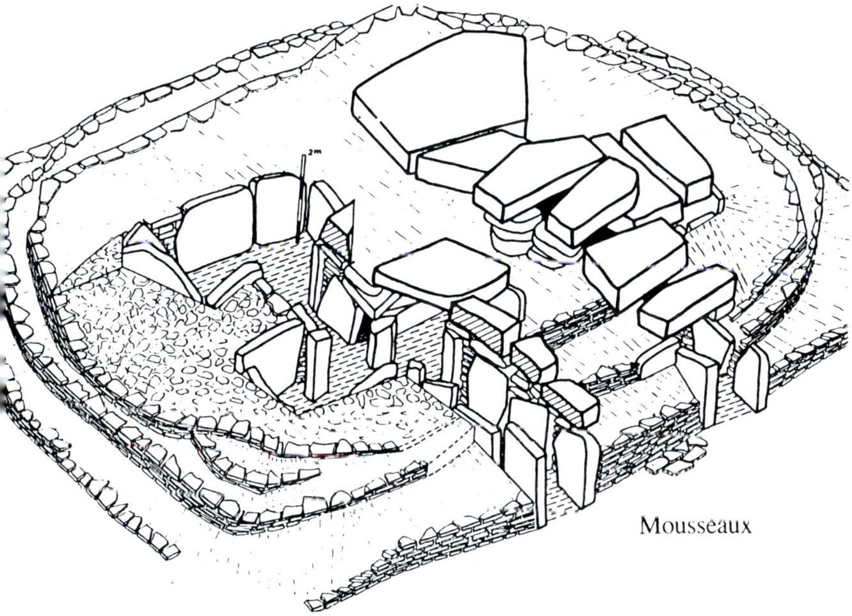

Mousseaux

DOLMEN OF THE MOUSSEAUX

District of Pornic, Loire-Atlantique

On the main hill the village of Pornic spreads out a megalithic group comprising the tumulus of the Trois Squelettes du Moulin de la Motte and the Mousseaux. This last one, explored in the last century, was made the object of a restoration in 1975-1977. It's the same type of transeptal dolmen containing lateral closets. Grave A, to the south, possesses a lateral closet on each side of the corridor and a large rectangular chamber. Grave B, to the north, is asymmetrical with only one lateral closet and one chamber in F with only one loge to the north. The monument was surrounded with small walls of drystone shelved in two levels. An abundance of funeral pottery was discovered there, round-bottomed vases, decorated incense-burners, pottery in concentric hoops of the Morbihannese of Castellic type. The neighboring tumulus of the Trois Squelettes and of the Moulin de la Motte, today hidden on private property, belong perhaps to the same cultural context. Pointing out also some ax engravings.

THE JOSELIERE DOLMEN

District of Clion-Pornic, Loire-Atlantique

The coastal length in the south-east of Pornic, several megalithic monuments dominate the sea. The Joseliere dolmen was restored recently by J. L'Helgouach. It was built in slabs in somewhat irregular tertiary stoneware with, at the entrance of the corridor, a fat block of white quartz. It includes a dolmen with antechamber with two lateral closets, one on each side, and a large rectangular chamber at the end. It is again an example of transepted sepulchure with lateral closets and cairn propped-up by small walls in drystone.

Some hundred meters further south of la Joselière is found still another transepted dolmen that of Prédaire or of la Boutinardière, equally built of slabs of tertiary stoneware. All of these monuments show that in the final Neolithic Age some regional groups distinguished themselves by the original architecture of their megalithic sepulchers.

La Joselière Dolmen. Photo P. Réveleau

The menhir of Champ-Dolent. Photo J.P. Gisserot)

DOL-TRESSE

To the south of Saint-Malo is a series of gallery graves and of menhirs of which two monuments are particularly interesting.

MENHIR OF CHAMP-DOLENT

District of Dol de Bretagne, Ille-et-Vilaine

2 km to the south of Dol, the beautiful menhir of Champ Dolent (the field of Pain) rises up its imposing mass to 9.50 m in height. It is in granite, which supposes a transport of less than 4 km. It shot up, as legend has it, in the middle of two armies in order to separate the two leaders who were brothers. It is said also that it sinks an inch each century and that it disparition will mark the end of the world. It is one of the largest menhirs in Brittany. Its faces have been carefully regularized with quartz or dolerite strikers. At the foot a fat block of dolerite, green-black in color, takes part in propping up the menhir and could have a spiritual role.

LA MAISON DES FEINS

District of Tressé, Ille-et-Vilaine

On the edge of the Mesnil Forest, to the west of the Tressé borough, hides the attractive gallery grave of La Maison des Feins (les Fées) (House of the Fairies) restored in 1931 by an English patron, Sir Robert Mond. A length of 12 m, it possesses still 7 covering slabs. At the end of the funeral chamber is found a small uncovered cell. The slab at the end of the door bears a figuration of two pairs of breasts which unfortunately a sex maniac lost control of his tool around 1960! On the slab to the right another working of two breasts rests intact. In each case under the breasts to the right is placed a necklace. One finds here again the double figuration of the goddess-mother, perhaps mother and daughter, goddesses of the harvest and the dead, the memory of which lasts in greco-latin mythology.

Gallery grave of Tressé . Photo J.P. Gisserot

Inside of La Roche aux Fées

Essé (Dolmens-Loire type)

THE ROCK OF THE FAIRIES

District of Essé, Ille-et-Vilaine

The Fairies played a large role in the megalithic legendry. The Rock of the Fairies often point out dolmens or gallery graves. In Ille-et-Vilaine it was the House of the Fairies or the Four des Feins. The Rock of the Fairies of Essé is the most celebrated. This enormous dolmen is constructed in fat slabs of red, cambrian shale on a local subsoil with small plates of green briovériennes shale. The closest layer of red shale is 4 km in the Theil Forest. It was of course the Fairies who transported the blocks in their aprons, losing one or more in the process. It is the little menhir of Runfort. The modern experiences of transport like the one realized in Bougon, Deux-Sèvres, showed that with 300 well-disciplined people, thick logs of wood and levers in the form of trees one could manipulate already sizeable slabs on the order of 40 tons.

The Rock of the Fairies is found on a summit, again a will to affirm its hold on the territory by the edification of a impressive sanctuary/grave. The monument measures 19.50 m in length and is oriented north-north-west-south-south-east which permits, at the winter solstice, the observation of the rising of the sun within the axis of the chamber. Three parts distinguish themselves in the architecture. To begin with a monumental portico is formed of an enormous squared-off block of 5.5 meters in length laying on two massive quadrangular pillars of 1 meter in height. Then, an antichamber of 3.50 m in length with three lateral slabs which contact with the principal chamber by a door made narrower by two transversal slabs. The principal chamber of 14 m in length, 4 m in width and 2 m of internal height. Three fat transversal slabs permit to fix the boundaries of four spaces within this chamber, perhaps "little family caves" although one might hesitate for such a monument between a role of temple and a role of funeral. More importantly, it was "emptied" early at the time of the roman era as is tesified by the fragments of border tiles frequently at this perimeter. The monument is implanted in a tumulus of brick pieces and was perhaps covered partially at the beginning until mid-slab or higher.

The Rock of the Fairies is typical of the series of angevin dolmens or the Loire type constructed in abundance in the Maine and Loire like that of Bagneux near to Saumur. These monuments are often composed of enormous slabs of calcium. They served without a doubt as sepulchers are dated by their pottery from 3,500 to 3,000 B.C.

By its natural environment, the Rock of the Fairies is one of the most beautiful dolmens in France. It has some small cousins in Brittany.

La Roche aux Fées

La Roche aux Fées

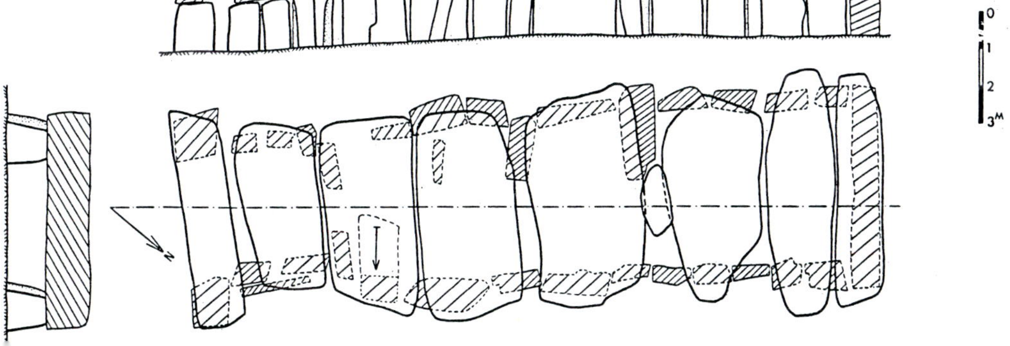

LA VILLE AU VOYER

District of La Chapelle-Caro, Morbihan

500m to the north of the village of La Ville au Voyer, a dolmen called La Maison Trouvée if not la Maison Trouée was the den of the Folliards, supernaturals who substituted themselves as babies. But in throwing nine gold-colored apples in a caldron, the spell was cast! La Ville au Voyer has a short hall of two lateral slabs with, at the entrance of the main chamber, two pillars where one has a slot for the laying in of a door. The chamber is covered by a unique slab of sandstone of 4.30 m in length and 3 m in width. It is an variant of the dolmens originating in the Loire. One ignores the materials which has been collected. The monument, situated in a small wood, is surrounded by a tumulus of small bricks of importance with some twenty meters in diameter. In the neighborhood several nice gallery graves are known like the one of la Chapelle-Saint-Méen, 1km to the west of the Ville au Voyer.

La Ville au Voyer. Photo : J-P Gisserot

THE COURNON TABLETS

District of Cournon, Morbihan

To the south of the village of Gacilly, in a pine wood overlooking the eastern shore of the Aff Valley, the Tablets of Cournon are another type of Loire dolmen. A length of 5 m and width of 2.70 m it possesses two large covering tables in pudding stone which come from a distant clearing 2 km to the east. The chamber is separated by transversed partitions and unfortunately reinforced by large pillars in Beton concrete

The Cournon tables. Photo : J-P Gisserot

The line of Druids. Photo : Jacques Briard

put into place previously in order to avoid a collapsing of the cover. A modern restoration is envisaged.

In the area of moors in Lanvaux several dolmens are connected also to the Loire type: The Follets in Saint-Gravé and Coëtby in Trédion, but, without a guide, they are quite difficult to find...

THE FOREST OF FOUGERES

The forest of Fougères is interesting because of the presence of entranchments like the oppidum of Poulailler dating from the Iron Age but also because of some megalithic monuments. There are some destroyed perhaps previously which are dificult to interpret like "The stone of Trésor", an enormous granite slab of 3m by 2m and 1m thick. It lays in a basin made deeper by treasure hunters, but also other monuments are original.

THE LINE OF DRUIDS

District of Landéan, Ille-et-Vilaine.

To the right of the road and at mid-trail of Fougères in Landéan is marked the "Line of Druids " again an abusive Celtisation of a megalithic monument. It is today a long line of 80 blocks of quartz spreading itself out over 300 m in the direction of north-north-east. The line is somewhat winding, many blocks of a small size or reversed. The line of menhirs developes itself essentially to the north of the forest trail but there are some blocks to the south, in disrupted positions. One has followed outside of this line of complementary enclosures which have disappeared in our time. The large alignments in a lone line are rare in Brittany but one can cite the one of Bocadève in Saint-Just, Ille-et-Vilaine and the one of "Noce de Pierre" in the the Swamps of the Devil at the foot of the Mont-Saint-Michel-de-Braspart. On all of these alignments the symbolic color of white was used.

The courcoulée Stone. Photo J.P. Gisserot

THE COURCOULEE STONE

District of Landéan, Ille-et-Vilaine

This beautiful gallery grave still called Stone of the Huguenots, souvenir of the religious wars, is found in the region south-west of the forest nearly 1 km to the south of the oppidum of Poulailler. It is constructed in fat blocks of rounded granite and possess still 12 pillars and 2 covering parts perhaps coming from one sole slab which was broken by treasure hunters. Its surrounding mound is still visible with some bordering slabs. This short gallery grave measures 6 m in length for 1.30 in width. Their funeral furnishings,which are far to dilapidated, are not known.

Several gallery graves are known in the region of Fougères. Those which come to mind are Rocher Jacquot 2km to the south-east of Saint-Germain in Cogles which are made up of a group of two gallery graves. Recovered there was a Chalcolithic brass knife (2000 B.C.)

Gavrinis and Er Lannic

The golf of Morbihan is rich in megalithic monuments distributed on it's banks and on it's islands. At Moines Island one can see the megalithic enclosure of Kergonan or the dolmen of Pen-Hap. The Longue Island possesses a handsome dolmen in tholos and with antechamber with engravings of goddesses but one cannot reach them. But the most important monuments are those of Gravinis and Er Lannic.

GAVRINIS

District of Larmor-Baden, Morbihan

A boating service starting at the port of Larmor-Baden or even at Locmariaquer allows one to reach the Island of Gavrinis but because of the fragility of the monument's engravings a restriction was imposed to the number of visitors (Find out in advance).

This "Island of the Goats" where certain adventurous thinkers see a connection between the goat Amalthea who nourished Jupiter and an island of 14 hectares on which is a small farm and which was in earlier times the place of a monastic establishment of Templiers. But it is to the south of the island, a little down below, that the clebrated cairn of Gavrinis is located which was saved by the intervention of the first inspector of Historical Monuments, the famed novelist Prosper Mérimée. Some work of Z. Le Rouzic restored the monument in a basic fashion before a modern campaign of rescue lead by C.-T. Le Roux in the years following 1980 revealed its architectural secrets.

Gavrinis is a classic dolmen with antechamber with rectangular chamber. The modern excavations have shown that the monument was prepared with thick, high ceilings of drystone arranged in tiers with a large facade of 28 m in length.

The long corridor of 11.80 m is prepared of 23 totally engraved slabs the same as the six slabs of the rectangular chamber of 2.70 m by 2.30 m. A complete covering with slabs by deep slotting recaptures the classic terms of megalithism: goddess-mothers in repetitive concentric hoops, axings, serpents, undulating signs, herringbone patterns (chevron), U-shaped signs (bovine?), hooks. In earlier times, certain authors saw on these as signs of fingerprints. But the comparison with the other monuments show well that above all it was a matter of a repeated theme of the goddess-mother. The innovations in excavation in 1980 were in discovering engravings on the outside of the

Gavrinis
Photo : J-P Gisserot

Engravings of Gavrinis
Photo : H. Morzadec

corridor and the chamber. In particular, the covering slab of the chamber bears an engraving of bovine with ploughs which, curiously, is reminiscent of the one at the Table of the Marchands in Locmariaquer. In order to cover 3 chambers of the Morbihan dolmens, the Gravinis one, that of Er Grah and the Table of the Marchands a large menhir of 14 m in height was engraved and then reduced in three blocks found in the modern age the study of which shows the perfect agreement by the nature of the granite, the look of the broken pieces and the junction of the engravings. It is an exceptional contribution to the study of the neolithic ritual.

THE CIRCLES OF ER LANNIC

District of Arzon, Morbihan

The currents of the golf of Morbihan are violent, which renders the entrance to the little island of Er Lannic difficult. However, one can notice by the boat which leads to Gavrinis the two circles of stones, one on the island, the other half-submerged in the sea. It is a unique example of the variation of the sea level since the Neolithic Age and also a somewhat rare example of the circles of mehirs in Brittany. The monument was searched by Z. LeRouzic from 1923 to 1926. The northern circle at 65 m in diameter and comprises blocks of 2.5 m to 5 m in height. The immersed group is in the form of an open iron horse to the east. It has a diameter of 61 m. The group contains some 60 stones 32 of which for the southern circle. Many have been revealed by Z. LeRouzic. Certain menhirs are implanted on an enclosure of small stones and earth, as with the circle of Ouessant, Finistère. Some numerous foyers and relics of habitats accompanied the menhirs, as well as some silex and numerous pottery including decorated vases, perhaps incense-burners of the "chassian" type, datable to 3,500-3,000 B.C. The monument must have played the role of astronomic temple landmarking the rising and setting of the moon and sun.

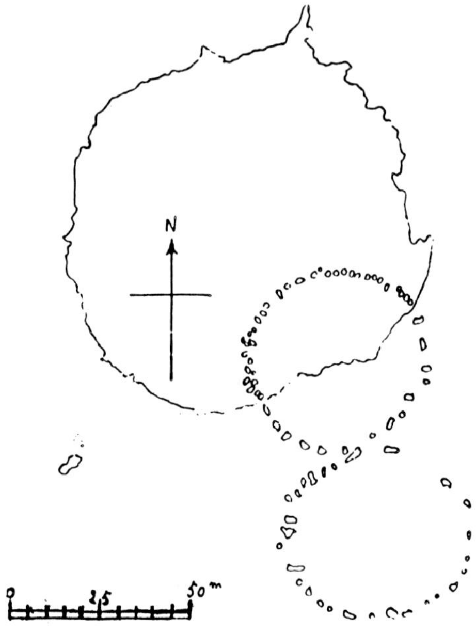

Plan of the cromlechs of Er Lannic in 1866 by Dr Closmadeuc

LANISCAT MUR-DE-BRETAGNE

The neolithic establishment in the inside of Brittany was due to the search for new territories to cultivate for the young generations but also for the presence of natural resources. Thus the dolerite of Plussulien, Côtes d'Armor, a very hard volcanic rock, was exploited on the hectares for the fabrication of some attractive axings. These axings products of the years 3,500 to 2,000 B.C. were exported in Europe as far as Belgium and England. These populations built for their dead some amazing megaliths on the neighboring crests of the Plussulien region.

NECROPOLIS OF LISCUIS

District of Laniscat, Côtes-d'Armor.

Three variants of gallery grave are known on the slaty crest which dominates the picturesque gorges of Daoulas where the Blavet flows. It is reached by the village of Liscuis, but sometimes a little patience is needed in order to find these three beautiful dolmens in the midst of the moor.

Liscuis I is a sepulcher in the shape of a V with a narrowed entrance. It is found a little below the crest down towards the Blavet. With a length of 12 m it opens with a narrow vestibule separated from the main chamber by a slab placed at an angle which leaves a small triangular "cat's hole". The gallery grave has three covering slabs. It was equipped with internal pavement on which was placed the funeral furnishings, neolithic vases and polished axes. A radiocarbon dating puts it at 3,190 B.C. The gallery grave is included in the cairn carefully realised in tablets of shale.

Liscuis II is a classic gallery grave of 15 m in length opened to the north, separated in one chamber of 8.5 m in length and an antechamber of 2.5 m. The separation is constituted of a notched slab which was sealed by a piece of triangular shale yet in place. Large bars of shale form a very neat paving. On the contrary, the surrounding mound was constructed more irregularly. This monument no longer has a covering table, the others having been without a doubt exploited by the quarrymen. The radiocarbon datings are from 2,500 to 2,200 B.C.

Liscuis III is also a classic gallery grave to the east this time and which possesses a small terminal cell with its covering slab. The pavement is irregular and was disturbed by foyers and perhaps by the installation of a sepulcher later on. The distinction of this monument is the presence in the eastern portion of a facade in slabs of shale which precede the surrounding cairn. These three monuments, restored by C.-T. LeRoux after the years of 1973 in conjunction with the dolerite workshops of Plussulien, show that on the same site some different architectural solutions could have been put into work.

The Laniscat group is typical of mégaliths of the final Neolithic period of interior Brittany. Other gallery graves are known in the same region like the one which is very ruined of Kerivoelen in Plélauff. The collected pottery in all of the gallery graves are quite rough, often in the form of a flower pot, analogous to the one of the Seine-Oise-Marne civilisation of the parisian Bassin.

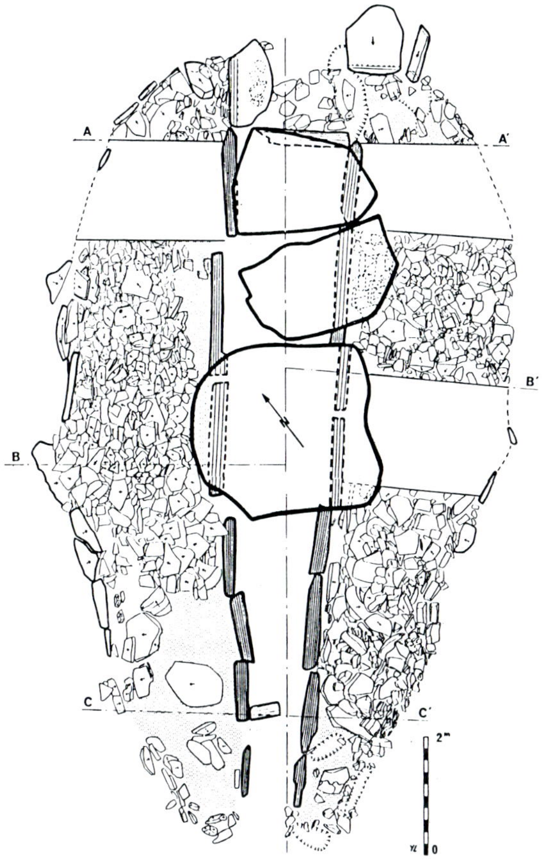

Liscuis I

Following pages:

upper left, Liscuis n° 2.
Photo J. Briard

and

Three views of Liscuis.
Photo J.-P. Gisserot.

Liscuis n° 1. Photo J.Briard

BURIAL OF COET-CORREC

District of Mur-de-Bretagne

Lateral entry of Coet-Correc.
Photo J. Briard

20 km to the west of Loudéac one must reclimb the dominant crest of the valley in order to find a nice burial with lateral entrance and porthole slabs between the lateral corridor and the chamber. The monument, length of 12 m, had the distinction of being christianized by the addition of an enormous portico in slabs of shale holding a crucifix. It is at this moment in the process of being restored. The burial has 6 covering slabs. The porthole slab which closes off the corridor is composed of two notched and joining elements.

The Côtes d'Armor are rich in gallery graves and burials with lateral entries. One can cite those of la Couette in Ploufragan, of Champ-Grosset in Quessoy or still the group of three gallery graves of la Roche-Camio, of the Petit-Chêne and the Ville-Glé pointed out to an archeological group of Plédran by a school teacher. All of these monuments attest to the denser occupation of interior Brittany by the populations of neolithic farmers.

Modern portico of Mur de Bretagne .
Photo J. Briard.

LOCMARIAQUER

The region of Locmariaquer is still one of the highest places of Armorican megalithism. The abundance of funeral monuments and their variety are impressive. Here, again, many monuments were saved by a narrow margin. The restorations were ventures by Zacharie LeRouzic which permitted the salvage of the essentials. After a period of stagnation, if not abandon, the monuments were made the objects of large salvage campaigns and appraisals in recent years. The modern excavations brought unedited and surprising information on megalithism. One can only call to mind here a few amongst the most typical monuments of this privileged area.

TUMULUS OF MANE-ER-HROEK

District of Locmariaquer, Morbihan

500 km to the south-east of the borough of Locmariaquer this enormous mound of stones of 100 m by 60 m reaches 8 m in height. In 1863, it was excavated "in crater" by the pioneers of the Polymathic Society of Morbihan which discovered in the center of a rectangular sepulchral vault with entrance a broken, engraved stele. The furnishings were made up of an extraordinary series of axings and pendants of precious stones, now the glory of Vannes's museum. The descent into the funeral crypt is made by a modern stairway where one can observe to the right the engraved slab, re-erected, with the badgal figuration of the goddess-mother and an array of U-shaped signs and polished axes. The Mané-er-Hroëk belongs to the great carnacean tumulus, of which another variety, the Mané-Lud, is found at the entrance of Locmariaquer. It is a mound of 100 m in length which contained small coffins and at its eastern end, a galleried dolmen famed for its engraved slabs of goddesses, axings and figurations of boats with oars.

Stele of Mané-er-Hroëk

THE TABLE OF THE MARCHANDS

The Table of the Marchands belonged to a certain era and to a certain family by the name of Marchand. Afterwards, one added an "s" to Marchand believing that it behaved as a meeting place for shopkeepers!

For a long while, the silhouette of this dolmen was that of an enormous table laying on 3 pillars. It was celebrated for its engravings on the rear slab with its hooks sometimes interpreted as a part of a wheat field. This engraving becoming damaged was recovered by Z. LeRouzic with an artificial cairn, much to the vexation of the inhabitants. Modern excavations have permitted the discovery that the monument was surrounded with a cairn with double facings, to become familiar with the new engravings on the outside and under the monument, the relics of the use of wood posts. The Table of the Marchands is a classic dolmen with antechamber.

The Table of the Marchands. Photo : J-P Gisserot

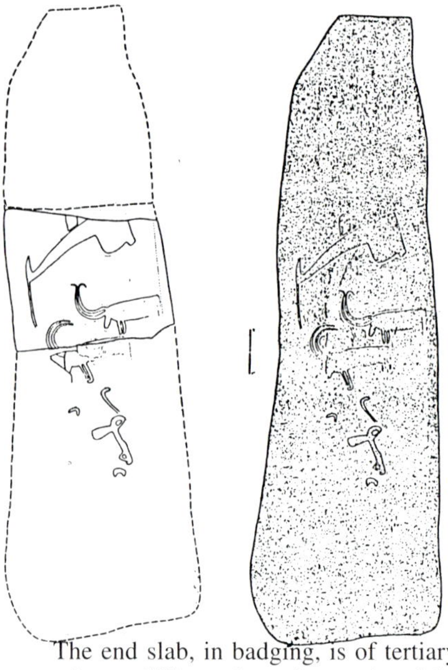

The end slab, in badging, is of tertiary sandstone different from the granite of the cover, granite which came from the Sarzeau peninsula.

This covering slab shows a figuration of hatchet-plows drawn by bovine of which only the hind legs are detailed. It is known now that this slab is a piece of an enormous engraved slab of cows and hatchet-plows; a large menhir which was broken in three in order to cover three different dolmens: the one of The Table of the Marchands, the one of Er Grah, the neighboring monument of the Table of the Marchands and the celebrated dolmen of Gavrinis. Modern observations by J. L'Helgouach have shown that other dolmens of Locmariaquer have also been covered with broken menhirs, in particular, the Mané-Lud and the Mané-Rutual, this striking dolmen situated in the middle of the borough of Locmariaquer.

THE GREAT BROKEN MENHIR

District of Locmariaquer, Morbihan

This giant of the menhirs of Brittany reaches more than 20 m for a weight of 350 tons. It lays in four enormous pieces. It was considered as the central element of an astronomic system regrouping the monuments of Carnac and Locmariaquer. It is believed also that it was knocked down by an earthquake or by lightening. Modern studies have given another interpretation; that the Neolithic people themselves cut up an engraved menhir in order to cover some dolmens, a theory substantiated by the disovery of an agreement between the engravings of Gavrinis and the Table of the Marchands. In addition, if one observes the position of the blocks, one notices that the western portion is already in the path of displacement, on the other side. Finally, the menhir bears on its second piece a very eroded engraving of a hatchet-plow. It, then, played a part in the "fallen idols" unveiling thus, the complexities of neolithic funeral rites.

THE FLAT STONES DOLMEN

District of Locmariaquer, Morbihan

The oldest dolmens of Locmariaquer are those with antechamber like the Mané-Lud, the Mané-Rutual or the smaller monuments like those of Kercadoret and of Kerveresse, on both sides of the road from Locmariaquer to Crac'h.

In the recent Neolithic period, around 3,000-2,500 B.C., the dolmens transformed by the addition of lateral cabinets or even of layouts with bent elongated chambers at right angles. The Flat Stone Dolmen, situated on the edge of the sea at the end of the Locmariaquer peninsula, is a good example celebrated for its engravings. At the entrance to its chamber stands a "menhir indica-

The great Broken Menhir. Photo J.-P. Gisserot

The Flat Stones , (Les Pierres Plates). Photo J.-P. Gisserot

Engravings of the Flat Stones.
Photo J.-P. Gisserot.

nothing but a raised slab at the time of the first restorations. The dolmen, bent to 120° has a length of 24 meters. It is made up of a first corridor of 6 m, a small lateral closet on its western flank and a large chamber of 16 m widened at its end with a separating slab. The slabs are engraved from the entranceway. They are somewhat complicated figurations derived from the goddess-mother perhaps with multiple breasts. One also notes the figuration of "ribbings " in earlier times considered as palms if not of "scarabs" from an era when one saw many influences from the Egyptians. In reality, it was a matter of an evolution of the figuration of the neolithic goddess-mother of which one there are several other variations on the angled dolmens of Morbihan like the ones of Rocher in Bono-Plouguemelen, of the little bay of Goërem in Gâvres or still of Luffang in Crac'h. Here the goddess is transformed in curious figuration bringing to mind an octopus in the mediterranean style. This fascinating slab was therefore transfered to the Carnac museum to avoid its deterioration.

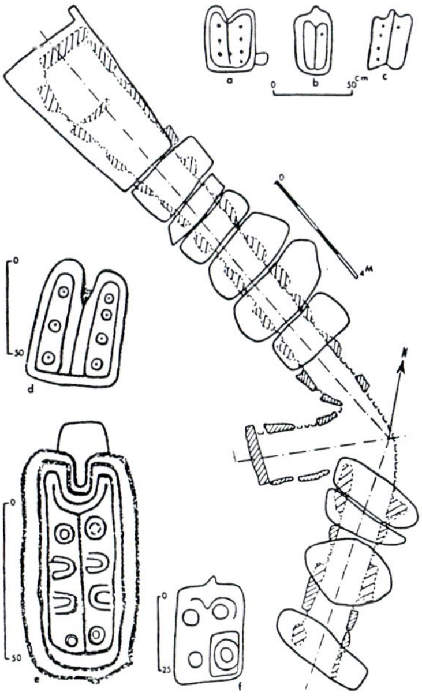

Ty-ar-Boutigued, Brennilis . Photo J. Briard

MONTS D'ARRÉE

In the heart of Finistère, the region of Monts d'Arrée was occupied from the first prehistoric moments. From there, some cut-out silex were gathered, from which numerous dolmens were built. Bronze Age people built there tumulus there in searching for metallic shelters like those of Huelgoat and the Gaulois where the large camp of Arthus was constructed.

TY-AR-BOUTIGED

District of Brennilis, Finistère

To the north of the borough of Brennilis, on the right after the village of Bellevue, is situated the original Ty-ar-Boutiged dolmen, a House of Korrigans, an example of V-shaped dolmens of J. L'Helgouach. It is included in an elongated mound which was bordered with slabs of which only the northern part is conserved. It is distinguished by a narrow entry (80cm) with a hall of 5 m uncovered and an enlarged part covered with three enormous granite slabs. A central pillar is erected there. The monument, oriented to the south-east, was violated very early on. Other dolmens of the same type, Keristin in Concarneau, Crugou in Plovan or le Rhun in Trffiagat, have given us pottery of the recent Neolithic period. Nearby monuments are known in Spain at Cueva de Menga, Malaga.

KERAMPEULVEN MENHIR

District of Berrien, Finistère

At the exit of Huelgoat, to the left of the old road leading to Berrien, the Kerampeulven menhir (the village of the menhir) stands in a shallow next to a waterway. Height of 5 m, it is regularized and thinned at its summit. It is the type of erect stone sometimes interpreted as a phallic stone. It is not impossible that this menhir may be late and a contemporary of the numerous tumulus of the Bronze Age abundant in the districts of Berrien, La Feuillée and Le Huelgoat. Other handsome menhirs in granite are standing in the same region, in La Feuillée notably. Also, one can note small dolmens where certain ones can be Bronze Age caves: Juno-Bella, La Croix-Pulviny in Berrien.

GALLERY GRAVE OF MOUGAU BIHAN

District of Commana, Finistère.

At 1.7 km of the town of Commana, after having crossed the route from Sizun to Feuillée, one enters the small valley of Mougau Bihan, at the foot of the crest of the Monts d'Arrée. At this place, rises one of the most beautiful gallery grave which has recently been restored. With a length of 14 m, it is to a north-south orientation. The 18 slabs of granite walls form a chamber 11 m length and 1,5 m in width. The southern portion of the monument possesses a small open cella separated from the chamber by it's headboard decorated with a superb axe formed in relief. At the middle of the chamber and near the entrance, four nother slabs carry figurations of "daggers" or of "death palettes". At the entrance of the chamber one the upper face of a pillar is a figuration of a pair of breast in relief.

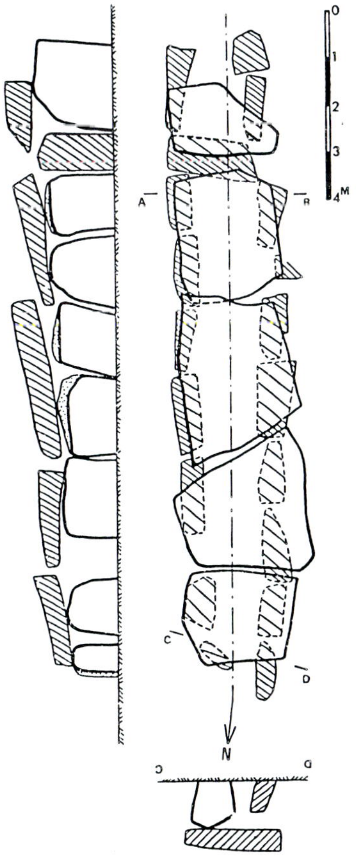

The Mougau Bihan. Photo J.P. Gisserot

Another slab possesses a double pair of breasts to the left of a dagger. in Commana, the goddess - mother looks, over at the entrance to the funeral vault, the peace and quiet of the dead.

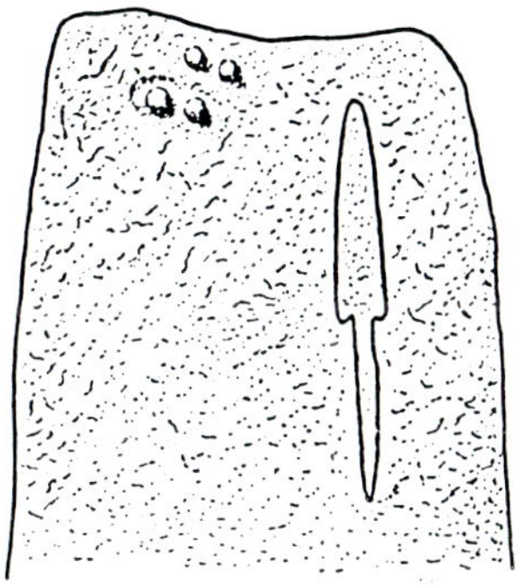

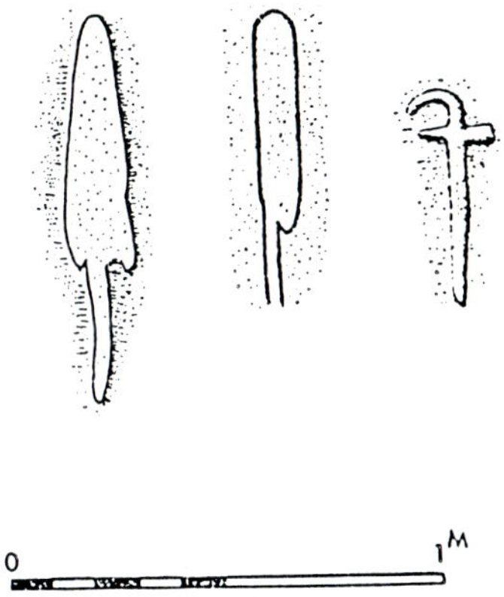

50

OUESSANT
Finistère

Megalithic Enclosure of Pen-ar-Lan

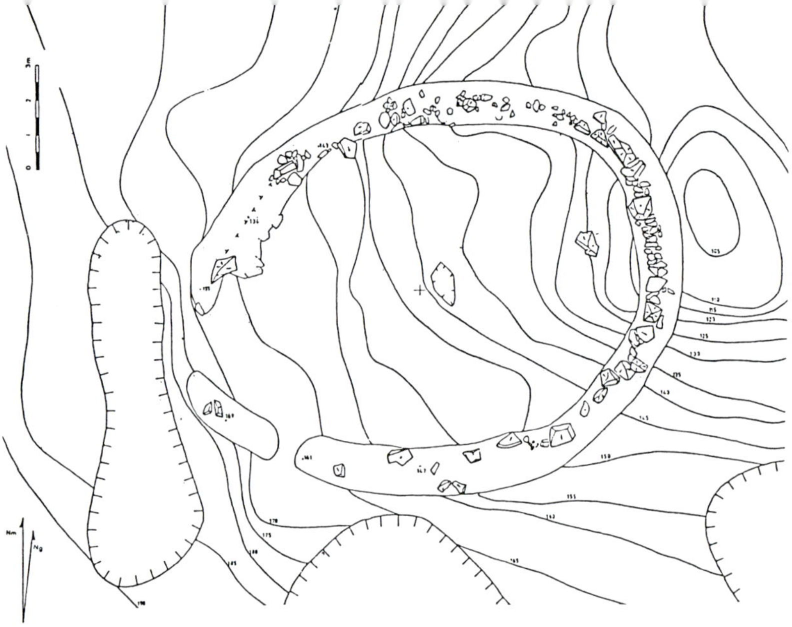

Ouessant, the island at the end of the world, has been known to have several megalithic groupings. One was described in the year 8 as a pagan temple by Admiral Thevenard. A watercolor by the painter Debret, around 1820, shows that it was a large quadrilateral of menhirs with a central, lengthwise separation. As time went on, the stones were taken away leaving nothing more than a few small menhirs on the neighboring embankment of the Creach lighthouse.

Another monument is found at the eastern end of the island at Pen-ar-Lan, after having passed the village of Kernoaz and near the cross said to be of Saint Paul. It is an enclosure of small menhirs, a "cromlec'h" of the old authors. It is oval in form, 13 m following the axis east -west and 10 m following the axis north-south. This monument was pointed out in the beginning of the century at a time where, at the center, was erected two little menhirs. This one has been taken since then. A salvage excavation lead in 1988 permitted the restoration of this little monument, probably an astronomic observatory permitting the location of the rising of the sun on the sea. The menhirs are in effect erected on a cliff of 23 m in height and is an excellent observation point. The excavation permitted the finding in the center the wedging pit of the central menhirs and a block which had been moved nearby was re-erected to this place in order to give an idea of the original monument. The monument is not alone, to the south a line of 4 menhirs gives a north-south alignment, completed by a perpendicular sys-

Ouessant. Photo J. Briard

tem running east-west at its end. In addition, 150 m directly east a quartz block could have been erected on its base marked by a hearth stone. Thus, it is so visible from the sea that marines repainted it in white so that it serves as a "seamark" ou spot for navigation! This might be a call back to its role in prehistoric times.

The circles of this type are abundant on the British islands and rare in Brittany where especially the immerged double circle of Er-Lannic in the Morbihan is known. It is this that makes the "megalithic egg" of the Ouessant interesting. Its astronomic role was monitored in 1988 by a series of investigations taken by M. LeGoffic on the day of a quite magnificent sunrise: June 21, day of the summer solstice. Each menhir could thusly mark the different sunrises during the course of the year, if not also the movements of the moon. It is a pity that the other groups of Ouessant have been destroyed. The island, situated at the end of known territory, must have played a particular role within the astronomic cult in Prehistoric times.

PLOUESCAT PLOUARZEL

The north coast of Léon, in Finistère, is sprinkled with prestigious or original monuments. There are first of all giant menhirs like the one of Brignogan, of Kerloas or of Kergariou, the highest in Europe, but also some gallery grave of which certain ones have the particularity of being found nowadays on the beaches, being covered by high tide and witnessing thus the rise of water since the Neolithic period.

GALLERY GRAVE OF KERNIC

District of Plouescat, Finistère

The Kernic creek is found 3 km west of Plouescat. On the northern beach is found one of the most beautiful gallery grave on Brittany with the relics of a large peristalith or entourage of granite slabs like the rest of the monument. This entourage, without a doubt, was modified by a laying out by wrackers in the East. The funeral chamber, oriented north-east-south-west, is a length of 9 m. It is separated by the head slab of an

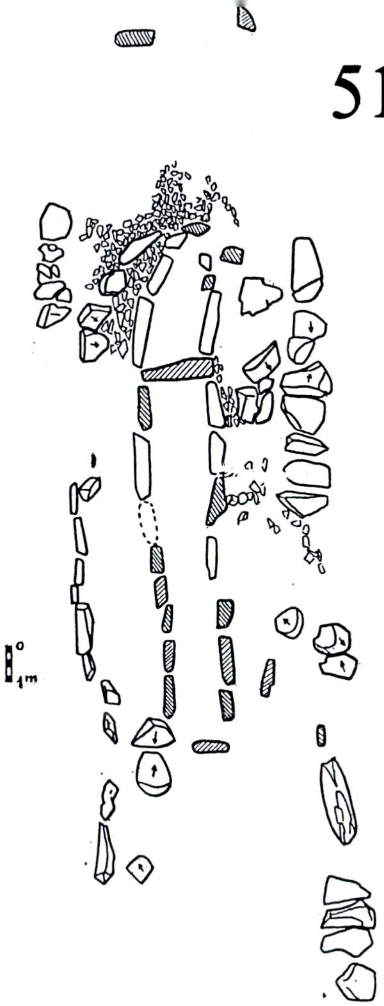

Gallery grave of Kernic in Plouescat. Photo J.-P. Gisserot

ending cella. In front of the south-east entrance traces remain of an esplanade which must have measured 8 m by 4 m and could have served as a ritual space. In 1983, the last excavations before its marine erosion permitted the finding of silex arrowheads and bell-shaped ceramics dating to the last use of the gallery graves around 2,000 B.C.

This monument is the most magnificent example of the variation of Amorican marine shores. Another example with gallery grave is known on the beach of Curnic in Guisseny.

KERLOAS MENHIR

District of Plouarzel, Finistère

This is the largest standing menhir known in Brittany. It measures 9.50 m from the ground but a violent storm destroyed the end of it some centuries ago and the knocked off pieces were collected from a neighboring farm. Its height must have exceeded 10 m. It is perfectly cut and it bears at its base on each side two lumps, in relief. This is a phallic symbol which was for a long while the object of superstitions. Future husbands would go there by night it is said and beat themselves against the protuberances unclothed in order to have beautiful children! The menhir is wedged by a blockage which was damaged some decades ago by treasure hunters. They left at the place debris of pottery which when collected afterwards proved to be carenean ceramics typical of the ancient Bronze Age, around 1,700 B.C. It is supposed that outside of its astronomic cultural role it could have served as location for the traders coming to find cassiterite, the tin mineral so abundant in this region of Saint Renan. One should note that this granite monster must have been transported over nearly 3 km beginning at the clearings in L'Aber Ildut.

The Kerloas menhir is not isolated. It could have been related with the two large menhirs of Kergadiou situated 8 km west in Plourin-Ploudalmézeau. One of these menhirs, standing, measures 9 m in height and is perfectly cut. The other, laying at an angle on the ground, is 11 m in length. These two menhirs form an alignment oriented northwest. These large menhirs of Léon could have constituted complex astronomic designs. Their size and transport are a perfect witness to their techniques of lifting. They are perhaps more recent, by their definition and perfect regularity, than the other giants like the one of Brignogan of which one face is rough, natural, and the other shows of the ripping off of rocks of its base thus being de-regularized after their being taken.

Kerloas menhir of Plouarzel. Photo M. Le Goffic

PLOUHINEC PENMARC'H

South Finistère was a very rich megalithic region but neverthless even here destruction for the development of the villages or the hunting by treasure hunters have disturbed this property. The point of Penmar'h and the Plouhinec region conserve nevertheless some interesting megaliths.

THE PENINSULA OF LA TORCHE

District of Plomeur, Finistère

This peninsula, on the road to becoming an island again as a result of the marine erosion, was occupied from the time of 5,000 B.C. by the megolithic fishers, who were great consummers of shellfish. At its summit is found an original monument, a long dolmen with closets probably lengthened in the recent Neolithic period by the addition of a corridor. Its position on this exceptional site dominates the bay of Audierne, in fact a place of privileged visit.

On the grounds in the east of the point of La Torche is found a dolmen with lateral closets of Kérugou which gave its name to an original ceramic of the Final Neolithic period characterized by streamlined vases ornamented in series of three vertical ribs.

Also note at the entrance to the borough of Penmarc'h the handsome Kerscaven menhir of which the channels of erosion have been compared with the folds of the garment of the Virgin Mary. Finally, situated at Saint Guénole, the Prehistoric Museum of Finistère regroups the most important prehistoric collection of Finistère.

Dolmen of La Torche Peninsula. Photo J. Briard

GALLERY GRAVE OF PORS POULHAN

District of Plouhinec, Finistère

The charming little fishing port of Pors Poulhan marks the limit between the bigouden countries and the one of Cap. On the cliffs which dominate to the west is found the group of compartmentalized dolmens of Souc'h, truly evolutionary dolmens in construction with the addition of successive rooms. Unfortunately, the maintenance of this wonderful group leaves much to be desired.

Another monument celebrated in earlier times was the gallery grave situated on the cliff between the port and the point of Souc'h. At the time of the last war its immense slabs obstructed the shooting of the german artillery and for this reason they were defeated. A patient job of salvage and restoration permitted M. Le Goffic to veritably revive this monument using photos, old sketches and proppings found again. It is a very beautiful long gallery grave of some 15 meters with an entourage of slabs ended in a point like the prow of a funeral vessel.

Aerial view of Pors Poulhan. Photo M. Le Goffic

Gallery grave of Pors Poulhan .
Photo M. Le Goffic)

Castel Ruffel in Saint-Goazec. Photo J.-P. Gisserot

SAINT GOAZEC GALLERY GRAVE OF CASTEL RUFFEL

District of Saint Goazec, Finistère

To the south of the Arrée Mountains, the Black Mountain holds some original monuments. The one of Castel Ruffel is one gallery grave with butressed pillars one against another, without covering slab. In order to reach the monument one must, starting at Roudouallec, take the road towards the north and at Coat Plain Coat go back up towards the large quarry. The gallery grave is there, often hidden by the ferns. The monument is intriguing for its enormous quartzite slabs. Legend has it that it was the house of a giant who lifted some of the slabs of the monument in order to throw them at the lout who stole his daughter! This original sort of construction is not unique in Brittany, among the other remarkable examples one can cite the gallery graves of Coat Menez Guen in Melgven, Goulet-Riec in Riec-sur-Belon and Lesconil in Poullan in Finistère. Found there also are some variants in the moors of Lanvaux in Kerfily in Trédion, Morbihan.

SAINT JUST LANGON

District of Saint Just, Ille-et-Vilaine.

The district of Saint Just, Ille-et-Vilaine, possesses one of the most remarkable groups of the interior megalithism in Brittany. The abundance of shale easily taken, the richness in lodes of guartz blocks are naturally a favorite of the construction of megalithic monuments. Its still not easy to distinguish the true menhirs which stand or lay down from natural blocks or simply ripped off the rock and left in its place or still some pseudo-menhirs erected here and there in the modern age in the middle of hamlets like the Roche-Mathelin. Some menhirs have also been displaced like the one of Bel-Air, repositioned to Pipriac in order to commemorate the heros of the Resistance. Some nice megalithic groups exist however like the one of Grée de Cojoux in the west of the borough which, from east to west, present an original takeoff point to megalithism in Brittany. But another dramatic problem has arisen these past years, the fires which ravaged the moors and the fields of pine in 1976 and 1989 notably, ruin the megalithic stones.

WINDMILL ALIGNMENTS

District of Saint Just, Ille-et-Vilaine

Nothing exists anymore of the old windmills of Saint Just except for a tower layed out in modern residence. The aligments are found down below the crest and spread out on approximately 400 m in three groups of lines of menhirs. A northern line includes some fifteen massive quartz blocks with crystalization, oriented to 105° north for

The alignments of Moulin in Saint Just. Photo : J.-P. Gisserot

115 m. They had been altered in the Bronze Age for the establishment of small graves of which one is a coffin with a very visible circular entourage. A southern line is composed of blocks of shale oriented 117° to north. The excavations of C.-T. Le Roux showed that there existed at their feet a veritable road of stones with post holes indicating that structures in wood complemented the menhirs, including a curious construction with four posts. The datings showed a construction terracing from 4,000 to 2,000 B.C. where the men of the Bronze Age deposited the ashes of their dead in an enormous pottery buried at the foot of the alignments. The group of Moulin is completed by a third line of menhirs with five massive blocks oriented to 15° north, perhaps perpendicular to the two first lines. One must follow its trail towards the west to discover it.

THE PINCHED YOUNG LADIES

District of Saint Just, Ille-et-Vilaine

Three young ladies dancing on the moor instead of going to vespers are transformed into stones by divine punishment. This little alignment, situated in the middle of Cojoux, makes up two blocks of quartz of 3 m in height and a third part lying on the ground.

Pinched Young Ladies in Saint Just .
Photo J.-P. Gisserot.

St Just. Le Château Bu (The Bu Castle). The Château Bu excavations are a unique example in Europe of a large mid-Neolithic dolmen - 3500 bc - covered with earth and used as a burial site in the early Bronze Age and surrounded by quartz menhirs - around 1500 b.c. Photo : J. Briard.

MONTENEUF

District of Monteneuf, Morbihan.

Until 1989, the erected stones of Monteneuf in Morbihan were only known as a few menhirs covered with ivy and hidden deep in the forest. Since then, Y. Lecerf's excavation campaigns uncovered 400 blocks of schist on scattered on a 6 hectare wide area. They are set on North-South and East-West alignments. They overlap older mounds and remains of quarries most of which date from prehistorical times. About forty of these blocks could be righted thanks to the position of their wedging, ressusitating a most interesting place of worship. It was probably destroyed and torn down in the early Middle Ages or around 1000 ac, when all pagans cults were chased. The rare elements of furniture collected range in date from early Neolithic to Bronze Age.

Photo : Nelson Martinez.

LE CHATEAU BU

District of Saint Just
Ille-et-Vilaine

The Bu Chateau or the Chateau of the Cow is this monument where, according to the legend, one sacrificed to God a beautiful heifer each year. It is a tumulus of 35 m by 25 m supporting four enormous blocks of quartz, one of which is lying down, with lines of small slabs in shale dug in vertically. The "treasure" hunters ripped it open in the center. It's a monument unique in Brittany of which the excavation permitted perhaps to make more precise the role of the temple or the tomb. One cannot come close to it except for certain circles in the British isles, some countries of Galles or Scotland, dating from the Neolithic Age to the Bronze Age. More to the east of the Chateau Bu is found the Tribunal, a demi-circle of menhirs facing an isolated block, perhaps the relics of a structure destroyed for building of the crest trail.

The Young Ladies of Langon. Photo J. Briard.

THE FOUR SARRAZIN

District of Saint Just,
Ille-et-Vilaine

At the western end of the moor of Cojoux, the Four Sarrazin still called the Little Owl Stones (les Pierres Chevêches), is a megalithic burial place where the entry must have been made to the side. The monument, 9 m in length, is set on a small lowered mound of 22 m by 7 m prepared with small slabs of shale on which one can see the sun, if carefully watched. One of the three covering slabs, fallen over inside, shows cupules or small circular indentations holding a ritual role. Also, one can find cupules on the neighboring rocks of Fort Sarrazin some 100 m north-east. Another nice gallery grave is known in Saint Just, the one at the Tréal moor, a wooded hill situated 3 km to the north-west of Saint Just. A length of 15 m, it is constructed in irregular blocks of puddingstone from Montfort with fat pebbles included on the rock. There are still 24 lateral slabs and some fifteen covering tables some of which have been disturbed by treasure hunters.

THE YOUNG LADIES

District of Langon
Ille-et-Vilaine

Langon is the small borough celebrated for the Saint agatha cathedral containing a roman fresco of Venus and heirs, but also by the "Young Ladies" again of shameless hussies transformed into stones. It is, on the main hill in Langon, an alignment comprising 6 rows of blocks of white quartz and 30 m to the north-west, the remains of a megalithic enclosure. The arrangement of the lines is north-west south-east. They are the last remains of an alignment which must have comprised a system of terminal enclosures like at Carnac, confirming the primitive importance of internal megalithism in Brittany.

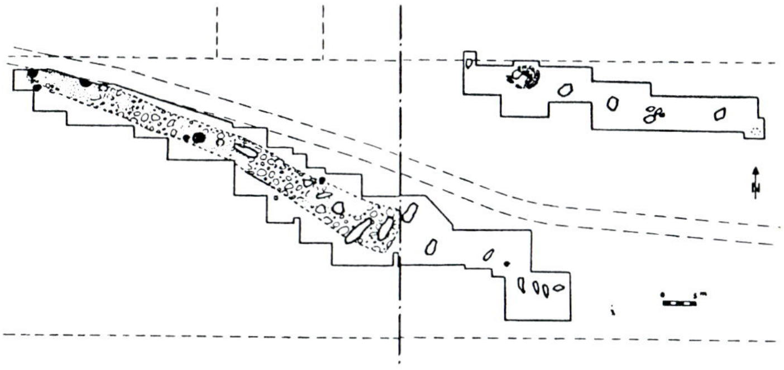

L'ensemble du Moulin

The Moulin group

TREGASTEL ST QUAY-PERROS

The pictoresque coast of rose granite was frequented intensively by the prehistoric population who found there abundant natural resources: slabs of granite for the funeral monuments, nodules of silex and pebbles for sets of tools, seafood and fish for food and even sea salt was mined in the ovens layed out on the beaches. In spite of the quarrymen and treasure hunters interesting monuments exist still, original by their architecture or their engravings. It is especially towards 3,000 to 2,500 B.C. that gallery graves and burial places with lateral entryways of the final Megalithic period multiplied.

BURIAL PLACE OF KERGUNTUIL

District of Trégastel, Côtes d'Armor

This monument, situated 2 km to the north-east of Trégastel, was excavated in 1939 by the local population who collected two collerette bottles of a type originating in Northern Europe. After the basic excavation, the four covering slabs in granite were put back into place on the monument composed of 7 lateral pillars on the south side and 6 on the north side. These here are very interesting by the presence of figurations of pairs of breasts in relief. The fourth slab starting at the east has six pairs side by side and the fifth slab two pair. Below the breasts figure some necklaces. One sees here the cult of the goddess-mother protectrice of the dead and the harvests. One reaches the inside of the monument by an artificial entrance corresponding to the missing slab of the north side. J. L'Helgouach classed this monument in the burial places with lateral entries and supposed that this entry should be situated in the south-east, on the current embankment. It has no terminal cella. On the same plot of land, is found a dolmen with an enormous table which served earlier as a residence home to a poor wretch who had layed out door and window.

GALLERY GRAVE OF PRAJOU-MENHIR

District of Trébeurden, Côtes d'Armor

The gallery grave of Prajou-Menhir is found to the left of the road leading to Penvern in l'île Grande between the sea and the swamp. It was included on an embankment. The monument is proceeded by a small menhir "indicator" 14 m away. It was excavated and restored in 1965. The covering is composed of 7 pretty granite slabs. The chamber, with a length of 9.50 m, is separated by a transversal slab interesting for it's engravings. They are of the goddess-mother, very stylized in rectangular cartons associated with the signs interpreted sometimes as daggers sometimes as "palettes of death". Also, there are a pair of breasts in relief with under-lying necklace and a double pair of breasts equally in relief, ones cut smaller than the others, a curiosity one finds also in Tressé, Ille-et-Vilaine.

Burial Place of Kerguntuil. Photo J.-P. Gisserot

Prajou-Menhir (foto di J.-P. Gisserot).

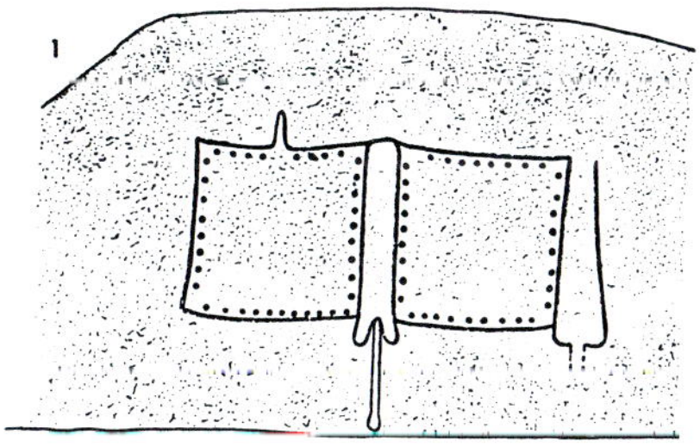

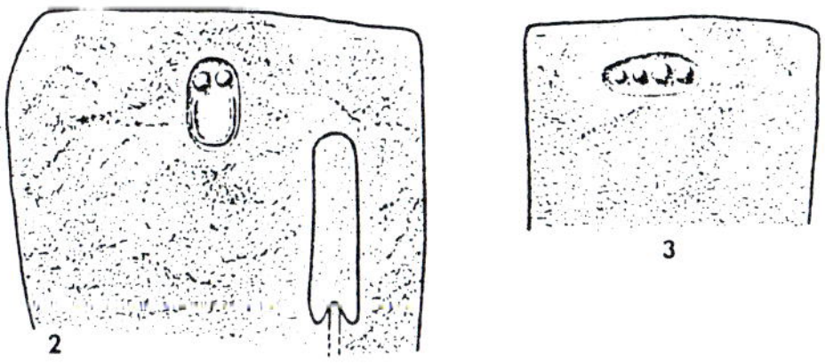

Engravings of Prajou-Menhir.

GALLERY GRAVE OF L'ILE GRANDE

District of Pleumeur-Bodou, Côtes d'Armor

This attractive gallery grave is found at the summit of the Ile Grande. A length of 9.5 m for 1.5 m in width it is covered by two long granite slabs. At a meter of the pillars of the gallery grave is found a peristalith or entourage of large slabs which reinforce the stability of the monument. It is probable that between these slabs and the gallery grave was found primitively a filling-up of earth or stones which have since disappeared nowadays. The density of the megalithic monuments of this region is surprising. One can cite other beautiful gallery graves like the ones of Renote Island and Milliau Island.

Goddess and dagger of Prajou-Menhir. Photo : J. L'Helgouac'h

MENHIR OF SAINT UZEC

District of Pleumeur-Bodou, Côtes d'Armor

The menhir of Saint Uzec (or Saint Duzec) is found on a small trail to the left of the road leading to the village of Penvern in Pleumeur-Bodou. This beautiful block of granite, height more than 8 m, bears on its rear surface channels of erosion where in earlier times one saw canals in order to make the blood flow of sacrificed victims! But the face, "before" of the menhir is remarkable for its christanization. A cross tops the menhir which bears at its summit, engraved in relief, the instruments of the Passion, the Saint Face, the Virgin, the Moon and the Sun. Earlier, on the same face had been painted a polychrome Christ which some post cards at the beginning of the century conserve as a souvenir. Several cases of christianization of megaliths are known in the Côtes d'Armor as much for the menhirs as for the dolmens. One of the most curious is the one of the Chapel of the Seven Saints at Vieux-Marché which keeps in its crypt the relics of a gallery grave.

Christianized Menhir of Saint Uzec. Photo J. Briard

BURIAL PLACE OF CREAC'H QUILLE

District of Saint-Quay-Perros, Côtes d'Armor

At 4 km to the north of Lannion, in a small pine wood to the right of the road leading to Perros-Guirec, is found one of the most exquisite examples of burial places with lateral entryways known in Brittany. Discovered in 1955, it was excavated in 1963-1964 by J. L'Helgouac'h. Its exceptional interest is in the conservation of its large surrounding mound of 28 m in length and 8 m in width bordered with slabs united by small walls in drystone. It is only missing the eastern end. The grave, with a length of 17 m, is decentered in the eastern part of the mound. The lateral entry is situated to the south. Just facing the entry corridor is erected an anthropomorphic stele with a pair of breasts and a necklace. One finds again here the neolithic goddess-mother watching over the dead. An abundance of ceramic furnishings going from the Final Neolithic Age to the Bronze Age was collected, in agreement with the radiocarbone datings of 1790 B.C. (end of the Neolithic) and 840 B.C. (end of the Bronze) obtained.

upper left: Creac'h Quillié in Saint-Quay-Perros . Photo J.P. Gisserot

lower left: Gallery grave of the Ile Grande. Photo J.-P. Gisserot

Saint-Quay-Perros,

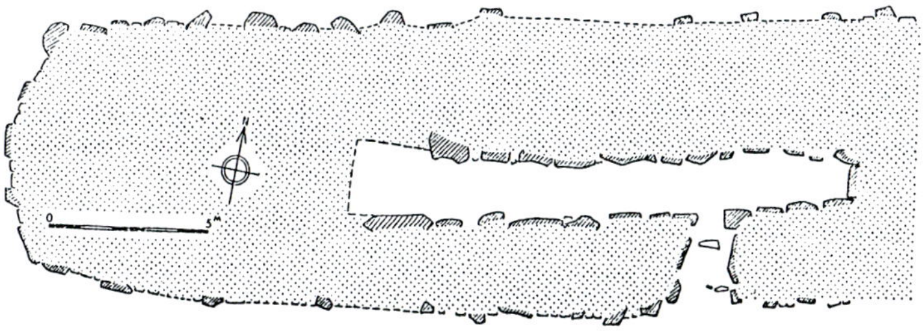

Côte des Abers et du Léon
Côte de Granit Rose
Trégastel
Île-Grande
Saint-Quay-Perros
Trébeurden
Pleumeur-Bodou
Lannion
Île Guennoc
Île Carn
Plouescat
Barnenez
Ouessant
Plouarzel
St-Renan
Brest
Morlaix
Commana
Berrien
Pte St-Mathieu
Camaret
Pte de Pen-Hir
Brennilis
Carhaix-Plouguer
Crozon
Châteaulin
Cap de la Chèvre
Baie de Douarnenez
Aulne
Canal de Nantes
à Brest
Douarnenez
Lac
Guer
Scorff
Saint-Goazec
Sein
Pte du Raz
Plouhinec
Quimper
Baie d'Audierne
Isole
Penmarch
Blavet
Quimperlé
Glénan
Lorient
Côte de Cornouaille
Erdeven
Groix
Carnac
Locmariac
Côte Sauvage
N
Belle-Île

Granville
Côte d'Émeraude
Baie de Saint-Brieuc
Cap Fréhel
Pte du Grouin
St-Malo
Avranches
Saint-Brieuc
Dol-de-Bretagne
Rance
Tressé
Lamballe
Dinan
Landéan
Canal d'Ille et Rance
Fougères
Couesnon
Rance
Rennes
Vitré
Paimpont
Ploërmel
Campénéac
Éssé
Monteneuf
la Chapelle-Caro
Vilaine
Saint-Just
Cournon
Langon
Canal de Nantes
Châteaubriant
Redon
Îles de Gavrinis et Er Lannic
Vilaine
à Brest
Sarzeau
Kerbourg
Côte d'Amour
Dissignac
St-Nazaire
Nantes
Pte de St-Gildas
Pornic
Lac de Grand Lieu

TABLE OF CONTENTS

INDEX OF PRINCIPAL SITES

Printed in France by Pollina s.a., 85400 Luçon - n° 42553